THE SPANISH STYLE HOUSE

From Enchanted Andalusia to the California Dream

THE SPANISH STYLE HOUSE

From Enchanted Andalusia to the California Dream

TEXT BY

RUBÉN G. MENDOZA

PHOTOGRAPHY BY

MELBA LEVICK

RIZZOLI NEW YORK

New York · Paris · London · Milan

*Dedicated to the inspired Spanish Colonial and Mission Revival
works of California architects Paul Revere Williams, FAIA (1894–1980)
and Julia Morgan, FAIA (1872–1957).* —R. G. M. and M. L.

First published in the United States of America in 2021 by
RIZZOLI INTERNATIONAL PUBLICATIONS, INC.
300 Park Avenue South, New York, NY 10010
www.rizzoliusa.com

© 2021 Rizzoli International Publications, Inc.
Text © 2021 Rubén G. Mendoza
Photography © 2021 Melba Levick

Publisher: Charles Miers
Editor: Douglas Curran
Production Manager: Kaija Markoe
Managing Editor: Lynn Scrabis

Designed by Scott Gross

Printed and bound in Bosnia and Herzegovina

2022 2023 2024 2025 / 10 9 8 7 6 5 4 3

ISBN-13: 978-0-8478-6516-1
Library of Congress Control Number: 2020942706

Visit us online:
Facebook.com/RizzoliNewYork
Twitter: @Rizzoli_Books
Instagram.com/RizzoliBooks
Pinterest.com/RizzoliBooks
Youtube.com/user/RizzoliNY
Issuu.com/Rizzoli

Cover: La Habra Heights, California. Original build 1929, 1935.
Remodel by architect Robert Sinclair, 2001.

Endpapers:
Zellij hand-cut tiles, Real Alcazar, Sevilla, Spain.

Opposite page 1:
Bougainvillea, La Habra Heights, California.

Pages 2-3:
Fountain, Palacio de Viana, Córdoba, Spain.

Page 5:
Bel Air Crest, California. Architect Robert Sinclair, 2006.

Pages 8-9:
Hacienda de San Rafael, Las Cabezas de San Juan, Sevilla, Spain.

TABLE OF CONTENTS

INTRODUCTION

The beauty, simplicity, and refined geometry of the art and architecture of Andalusia or southern Spain has inspired generations of writers, photographers, architects, artisans, designers, and interior decorators. Andalusia is heir to the melding of Romano-Iberian and Syrian, Byzantine, North African, Islamic Berber or Moor, and Arabic, Neoclassical, and Mediterranean through Iberian traditional technologies and architecture. These in turn constitute an Islamic legacy spanning some fourteen centuries. As such, the *al-Andaluz* or Andalusian tradition remains central to advancing those Spanish colonial and Mediterranean styles that continue to play a major role in the elaboration of contemporary architecture in California and the West. From the Spanish royal court of Queen Isabella and King Ferdinand in Segovia to the spectacular *Alcázar* or palisaded courts and Great Mosque of Córdoba—or the twelfth-century *Giralda* or *minaret* tower of *Sevilla* and the thirteenth-century royal palace and fortress of the Alhambra in Granada, the Andalusian style has long beckoned and inspired architects and designers. In search of the primordial traditions and techniques that produced some of Spain's most flamboyant and sophisticated architectural expressions, and by extension, Spanish architecture from throughout the Americas, we are drawn to the multitude of architectural features and elements that constitute the Andalusian tradition.

Massive earthen or adobe walls, gleaming white stucco, terracotta roof tiles, asymmetrical floor plans, curvilinear parapets, and masonry colonnades are the most notable features that define the tradition—a tradition borne of *Mudéjar* or Moorish artisans whose legacy lived on through their respective works long after the Spanish Reconquista of the whole of the Iberian Peninsula in 1492. The

(*Above*) Vejer de la Frontera, Spain.
(*Left*) Casa Santa Pola, Ronda, Spain.
(*Opposite page*) Vejer de la Frontera, Pueblos Blancos, Spain.

11

many regional variants of the tradition have in turn lent themselves to its identity through the addition of tiled arcades, charming patios and lush courtyards, solid wooden doors and gateways, wrought-iron embellishments, and towering chimneys and rock-cut fountains. All convey characteristic features of the Spanish traditions subsequently introduced throughout the Americas, and each regional expression in its turn drew inspiration from southern Spain and North African antecedents.

(Top) Ronda was built atop a Roman fortress.
(Bottom) Plaza de Toros, Ronda, Spain.

The Andalusian style in California first makes its appearance in the art and architecture of the Spanish and Indian missions of the region. Its expression most readily apparent in the extant mission churches of San Carlos Borromeo (1797), San Gabriel (1805), San Diego (1813), and San Luis Rey (1815). In each instance Neoclassical, Gothic, and *Mudéjar* art and architecture were distilled into hybrid forms. With the ruination of the California missions in the period after 1834, these same missions were recast and romanticized by the Americans as silent and forlorn sentinels of early Christendom in the West. By the late nineteenth century, they were the subject of a host of cultural initiatives devoted to historic preservation and heritage promotion. The late nineteenth century thereby prompted a Mission revival, along with related variants in Spanish Colonial Revival styles that took root in Southern California and Florida.

THE MISSION REVIVAL STYLE

The largest and most notable such Mission Revival style building on record was that of one Frank Augustus Miller of Riverside, California. Miller acquired the Glenwood Cottage built by his father in 1876. Under Miller's direction, the property rapidly evolved into the sprawling Mission Inn Hotel & Spa. The Mission Inn showcased architectural eclecticism centered on the Mission Revival style then in vogue. It then blossomed with the addition of some two hundred rooms in 1903. Construction continued under Miller's direction through 1931, by which time stylistic borrowings from each of the twenty-one California missions were integrated into the sprawling complex, including as it did such notable features as the Mission Wing, Cloister, Spanish Wing, and the Rotunda Wing. While boasting a leading place in advancing the Mission Revival style, in reality Miller's vision spanned a multitude of architectural revivals, not least of which included Spanish Gothic, Moorish, Spanish Colonial, Renaissance, and Mediterranean Revival styles. The popularity of the otherwise flamboyant Mission Inn attracted the film stars, celebrities, and political figures of the time, among the most notable being Harry Houdini, Mary Pickford, Bette Davis, Ginger Rogers, W. C. Fields, Clark Gable, Cary Grant, Spencer Tracy,

and US presidents Theodore Roosevelt, William Howard Taft, and Herbert Hoover. This fed into a national psyche bent on proclaiming the magnificence of the Spanish traditions of Andalusia and its richly textured histories in the wake of both the Spanish-American War of 1898 and the completion of the Panama Canal in 1914. Whether deemed Mediterranean Revival architecture like that of the Hayes Mansion Hotel of 1905 (in California's Silicon Valley), each of these revivals bore elements derived directly from the architectural styles identified with Andalusia and the skilled *Mudéjar* craftsmen and -women recruited to the Americas during the era of Spanish colonialism spanning the period from 1521 through 1821.

SPANISH COLONIAL REVIVALS

A number of developments converged in 1915 to bring Andalusian Spain to prominence in North America, and California architects and designers in particular. In that year, the people of San Diego determined to celebrate the dedication of the Panama Canal. At the same time, the world's fair came to San Francisco in the guise of the Panama–Pacific International Exposition. Thus, the world's fair was rivaled by San Diego's decision to launch its own world's fair in the form of the Panama–California Exposition of 1915. Unlike the San Francisco exposition with its predominantly perishable structures,

San Diego recruited noted New York architect and designer Bertram Grosvenor Goodhue (1869–1924) to design an exposition complex in Spanish Colonial Revival, and predominantly Andalusian, styles. These designs consisted of intricately embellished and durable masonry buildings that have endured the test of time. Touted as Gothic and Spanish Colonial Revival design, the exposition in San Diego's Balboa Park celebrated the completion of the Panama Canal, and thereby launched widespread and popular interest in the Andalusian mystique at the inception of its broader appeal as part of a Spanish Colonial Revival style design movement in California and the West (1915–1931).

The most prominent architects and purveyors of the Spanish Colonial and Mission Revival styles of the 1920s and '30s include George Washington Smith, Julia Morgan, Wallace Neff, Bertram Goodhue, Lilian Rice, John Byers, Myron Hunt, Gordon Kaufmann, Roland Coate, Paul Revere Williams, James Osborne Craig, and Mary McLaughlin Craig, among others. Two of the most notable, George Washington Smith and Julia Morgan, provide our point of departure for this exploration of the Andalusian-California connection.

GEORGE WASHINGTON SMITH

Enter Philadelphia architect and painter George Washington Smith (1876–1930), whose travels through Andalusia in 1914 proved instrumental to his subsequent career as an architect in California, and in particular, the Santa Barbara area. In 1915, Smith traveled to San Francisco for the preview of his paintings then on exhibition at the San Francisco Palace of Fine Arts. After a sojourn at the Panama-Pacific International Exposition, Smith traveled to Santa Barbara to visit friends in Montecito and to purchase land, all the while abandoning plans to return to Europe after the end of the Great War. In 1917, Smith designed and built his first home and studio in

(Above) Mission San Diego de Alcala, 1769, San Diego, California.

(Above) Sherwood House, George Washington Smith, 1928, La Jolla.

(Below) Andalusian inspired archway by George Washington Smith.

a style reminiscent of the Andalusian farmhouses he observed in his travels. Casa Dracaena (Dracaena House) or El Hogar (The Home or Hearth) was built at the Montecito site, and soon drew the fancy of his neighbors in Santa Barbara. So popular was the design that he dropped his painting career for one in architecture. Smith was credited with building some eighty such Andalusian or Spanish Revival style homes throughout the region, and further afield, in other areas of the US. Smith's devotion to the art and architecture of Andalusia was such that virtually all elements of the tradition appear in a number of those homes and estates that he designed.

JULIA MORGAN AND "THE ENCHANTED HILL"

Whereas George Washington Smith is known for his residential commissions in Santa Barbara County in particular, renowned architect and engineer Julia Morgan (1872–1957) designed some seven hundred buildings in California in the period spanning 1904 through 1947. Some of the most notable designs of Morgan were those that expressed the Mission, Moorish, and Spanish Colonial Revival styles of the time. Perhaps her most celebrated such works are those commissioned by newspaper magnate William Randolph Hearst, and identified with the *Los Angeles Examiner*

building, La Hacienda located within the confines of the former Hearst Ranch and adjacent Mission San Antonio de Padua; and La Cuesta Encantada (The Enchanted Hill), popularly known as Hearst Castle. Whereas Morgan designed the Examiner building in the Mission Revival style, a host of other projects, including both La Hacienda and the famed Hearst Castle were designed with a blend of Mission, Moorish, and Spanish Colonial Revival styles in mind. The opulent Hearst Castle, Hearst's private estate, is situated atop the "Enchanted Hill" overlooking the California coast at San Simeon. Morgan designed and oversaw construction of the massive cast-concrete complex of buildings. Its charter was predicated on the architectural and artistic styles and designs of southern Spain, and it was built in the years spanning 1919 through 1947.

Like its noteworthy predecessor, the Mission Inn in Riverside, the complex of buildings at Hearst Castle featured an eclectic array of Mission, Moorish, and Spanish Colonial Revival styles, and each was the result of cast-concrete construction methods. While both Frank Augustus Miller of the Mission Inn, and William Randolph Hearst at San Simeon each insisted on the integration of authentic Andalusian, Mediterranean, and other period artworks, Hearst's collections included architectural elements and monuments salvaged from some of the great churches and estates of southern Spain and Europe. Among the most notable features of the Hearst estate is that of the towering and majestic Casa Grande, designed by Morgan after the Andalusian church of La Iglesia de Santa María la Mayor, in Ronda, Spain. As with the Mission Inn, many of the celebrities and political elites of the time, including several US presidents, were hosted at the Enchanted Hill. Being the flamboyant publishing tycoon that he was, Hearst publicized the great works and the stirrings of the elite who alighted on the hill of the enchantments. Today, Hearst San Simeon State Historical Monument remains one of the most sought-after attractions in California, and draws nearly one million visitors each year.

(Left) Monasterio de San Francisco, Palma del Río, Spain.

AL-ANDALUZ AND THE ARAB LANDS

(Above) Casa de las Dueñas, Sevilla, Spain.

In 2011, the Metropolitan Museum of Art in New York recruited fourteen Moroccan craftsmen from Fez to handcraft a scaled-down in-house version of an Arabic courtyard, the Moroccan Court, replete with traditional Islamic and North African design considerations, materials and techniques. The resulting court now constitutes the centerpiece of some fifteen new galleries devoted to the art of the Arab lands, and represents but a microcosm of those achievements borne of some fourteen centuries of Islamic civilization. The intricacy, sophistication, artistry, and pride in the craftsmanship thereby elaborated upon to represent the millennial-old traditions of the Arab lands are palpable and at the same time hearkens to the opulence of the Islamic tradition.

As an archaeologist and architectural historian, I was lured back to the Metropolitan Museum of Art in July of 2019 with the expressed intent of experiencing the Moroccan Court. I had spent that month in Washington, DC, at the National Endowment for the Humanities Summer Institute, in a course called "Museums: Humanities in the Public Sphere," the Moroccan Court first came to my attention while resident at Georgetown University. Upon entering the Art of the Arab Lands exhibition space, I was readily drawn to the Moroccan Court, a particularly refined and contemplative space where I sat for hours on end admiring the finer details of each of those architectural elements identified with the Andalusian traditions brought to bear in that space by the master craftsmen from Fez.

While studying the artistry of the architectural features and embellishments integrated into the Moroccan Court, I was most taken by the elegance and symmetry, intermingled calligraphies, Koranic texts, sacred geometry, and the interplay of light and shadow. These intricately sculpted geometric designs and floral patterns proclaim through their very form a sense of connectedness, timelessness, and an infinite and continuous divine proportionality borne of pure abstraction, and symbolic and repetitive motifs. The aniconic designs generated as such were intended to avoid the representation of humans or animals as per the teachings of the Quran or Koran. When taken together, the central elements of the Moroccan-Andalusian

divine revelation is expressed through geometric and floral patterns or *arabesque* or islimi designs found in a variety of media, including glazed tile work, ceramics, and carved stucco arcades and cedar corbels. From marble chess pieces and Hispano-Moresque wares dated to the fourteenth and fifteenth centuries to *zellij* mosaic tile works, the Moroccan Court celebrates the fusion of North African and Andalusian art, architecture, and technology. It thereby serves to reify the artistry and integrity of a millenarian tradition that proliferated across those circum-Mediterranean lands united under the Islamic caliphate of AD 622 through 750. Through the course of the next several centuries, *al-Andaluz* achieved its most opulent and magnificent expressions on the Iberian Peninsula of the fourteenth through fifteenth centuries of the Common Era.

With the Spanish Reconquista of 1492, the Islamic caliphate was ultimately vanquished, and those Iberian Moors or Muslim artisans that remained behind were deemed *Mudéjar*, from *mudajjan*, or those "tamed" or "domesticated" under the rule of a Christian monarch. The extent, to which the Metropolitan Museum of Art has officially acknowledged the great works, and particularly the art and architecture of Islamic civilization, is writ large in this diminutive homage to a truly wondrous world tradition.

style expressed in this singular downsized version of a madrassa school or prayer court all come together in this re-creation at the Met. There at the center of the ensemble lies the scalloped marble fountain, glazed tile surround infixed into the marble flooring, a dado level composed in its entirety of *zellij* mosaic tile panels, stucco walls and hand-carved embellishments across the span of the arcade, cedar corbels, and glazed green roof tiles. The thirteenth- and fourteenth-century madrassas and palaces of Morocco and the Alhambra of Granada, Spain, inspired these elements.

The majority of those architectural elements, glazed tile works, and other artifacts housed in the Moroccan Court at the Metropolitan Museum of Art are sourced to the region of Andalusia and southern Spain. They effectively reveal those ancient and hybrid expressions that coalesced around the creation of the Moroccan-Andalusian style—a style whose mastery of the geometry and symmetry of

(Top left) Islamic Spanish column capital, tenth century, De Madinat al-Zahra, Córdoba, Spain.

(Above) Archaeological vestiges of De Madinat al-Zahra, Córdoba, Spain.

ANDALUSIAN ORIGINS

As a veritable crossroads for waves of conquering armies, intrepid mariners, and international merchants, Spain and the peoples and traditions of the Iberian Peninsula are the product of tens of thousands of years of momentous cultural achievements. These span native Iberian cultural origins, and the unrelenting onslaught of such groups as the Phoenicians, Carthaginians, Greeks, Romans, Vandals, Visigoths, Byzantines, Jews, Romani, Islamic Berbers or Moors and Arabs, and Castilian and other Christianized northern Iberian peoples. Each of these civilizations marked, radically transformed, or scorched the lands identified by Roman historians and geographers with *Hispania*, and each lent itself to the elaboration of the architectural heritage of the region. The Roman occupation alone introduced classical art and architecture, agriculture, urban planning, hydraulics, language and literature, and a host of technologies and industries. *Iberia*, or the Iberian Peninsula, was first referred to as such by Greek historians as early as 500 BC. The Roman occupation of the region produced such ancient towns, cities, and public works as those of the trading center of *Baelo Claudia*, the aqueduct of Segovia, and the port city of Tarragona. The Roman theater of Mérida, the walls of Lugo, and the bridge of Córdoba similarly introduced the Latin political and geographical names identified with *Hispania* and *Hiberia* (Greek: *Iberia*). As Latin synonyms, the former refers to the political designation of the Roman province as of 200 BC, whereas the latter connotes the geographic identification of the region with the "land of the Hiberians," or those of the 578-mile-long Ebro River, or *Hiberus* Much of that region later identified with Andalusia corresponds in large part to the southernmost and smallest of the three former Roman imperial and senatorial provinces that dominated the Iberian Peninsula in AD 117. *Baetica* constituted the Roman senatorial province of the era. The province's wealth and prosperity, and fealty to Roman lifeways, was rewarded by Emperor Vespasian with the granting of the *jus Latii*, thereby giving the rights and privileges of

(Right) The Ford House, Architect Paul Williams, 1929, Ojai, California.

18

Roman citizenship or *Latinitas* to the people of *Hispania*. Baetica was adjoined by the Roman imperial provinces of *Lusitania* on the northwest, and that of *Tarraconensis* on the north and northeast, and had the added advantage of spanning both the Mediterranean and Atlantic coastlines at the intersection with the Strait of Gibraltar and the Pillars of Hercules. Encompassing the ancient cities and ports of *Corduba* (Córdoba), *Gades* (Cádiz), *Hispalis* (Sevilla), and Italica (*Santiponce*), Baetica was soon transformed into the agricultural breadbasket and granary of the Roman Empire. This led to Baetica's production and exportation of precious metals such as gold and silver, as well as tin, lead, olive oil, wine, wool, wheat, fish, and the popular condiment *garum*, or fermented fish sauce. Olive oil production, and viticulture, or the cultivation and harvesting of grapes for wine production, were by far the region's single most important exports, and combined with wheat, they comprised the Iberian culinary triumvirate upon which Rome depended.

(Above) The Andalusian countryside.
(Previous pages) Coppell Mansion, architect Bertram Goodhue, 1915, Pasadena, California.

A succession of marauding warlords and rival nation-states swept into the vacuum left with the decline of Roman *Hispania*. Baetica's strategic location as the gateway to Europe, the Mediterranean, and North Africa was instrumental in its allure to a succession of émigrés and invaders alike. Among these are a brief interlude by way of which the Vandals traversed the region en route to North Africa, only to be followed in short order by the Kingdom of the Visigoths, who ruled the region from the late fifth through eighth centuries. And that despite the expansion of the Byzantine Empire that swept through the former western Roman province of Baetica, or *Spania*, and the Balearic Islands from AD 552–624. After a protracted period of internal conflicts and external threats, the Umayyad, or North Africans under the command of *Tàriq ibn Ziyad* and *Mussa ibn Nussayr,* spearheaded the Muslim invasion of the region in AD 711. The conquest of the Visigoths ushered in the establishment of an Islamic caliphate that dominated much of the Iberian Peninsula, and Andalusia in particular, from the eighth through fifteenth centuries.

El Andalucía first entered the Spanish language in the thirteenth century as a reference to those territories then under Spanish rule in a world dominated by the Muslims or Moors. The name has long been attributed to the Arabic pronunciation of the Gothic term *landa-hlauts* (land-lot), Germanic nomads or Visigoths swept into the Iberian Peninsula and thus dominated much of that region identified with Andalusia from AD 468 through to the Islamic conquest of 711. Their partitioning of land allotments administered by Visigoth lords followed the earlier Germanic pattern. An Arab coin, or *dinar*, minted within five years of the Arab conquest of the Iberian Peninsula in AD 716 features the first bonafide reference to the use of the term *al-Andalus* by way of a bilingual inscription bearing the names "Span(ia)" in Latin, and *al-Andaluz* in the Arabic.[1]

Today, Andalusia (*Andalucía*) is construed an autonomous community with a "historical nationality" rooted in a particularly strong and vibrant cultural identity. With its capital in Sevilla, the territory consists of eight modern provinces, including Almería, Cádiz, Córdoba, Granada, Huelva, Jaén, Málaga, and Sevilla. The three principal regions identified with Andalusia include the Sierra Morena, the Baetic Depression dominated by the valley of the Guadalquivir river, and the Cordillera Penibetica. The whole of Andalusia encompasses some 87,597 square kilometers (33,821 square miles), or 17.3 percent of the Spanish landmass. The region boasts the hottest and driest summers and wettest winters in Spain. A host of its traditions, including such colorful dances as that of the flamenco—song, dance, and guitar (*cante, baile, toque*)—the tenth-century version of the Persian game of chess (*shatranj* or *ajedrez*), the Palma del Río or Valencia oranges (*Citrus-naranja*), and to a lesser extent bullfighting (*corrida de toros*) are culturally identified with Andalusian origins. Ultimately, it was within such a geographical, cultural, and political landscape that the Hispano-Moorish or Andalusian architectural tradition first emerged as the principal signifier for all that the region represents.

ABOUT THIS BOOK

With some sixty photography books on architecture, travel, and design under her belt, internationally acclaimed photographer Melba Levick is no stranger to the world of fine-arts photography and the spirit of each of those places she has captured on film. I, Ruben G. Mendoza, am an archaeologist, photographer and architectural historian with expertise spanning the art and architecture of early California and the Viceroyalty of New Spain (Mexico). Perhaps it was no accident that we again met to commune over the world of photography and architecture; and that in the wake of our previous Rizzoli book, *The California Missions* (2018). With my long-standing interests in photography and architecture, and architectural histories of historic buildings in California and the West, this union of our common interests led to our first collaboration. No sooner had we completed work on our first book, Melba once again approached me about a new collaboration for a second, and even

[1] Barrucand, Marianne, and Achim Bednorz. *Moorish Architecture in Andalusia*. Madrid: Taschen, p. 12, 2002.

more compelling, book project concerned with those design sources that have long influenced California traditions both past and present. Having thoroughly interrogated the suite of design elements and styles identified from the California missions in our first book, it was clear that a common thread unites the architectural traditions of Andalusia via the Spanish missions through to contemporary California. Clearly, the stylistic currents of that earlier time have resurfaced by way of a protracted interest and resurgence in the "Spanish" styles of the late nineteenth and early twentieth centuries through to the present. The origins of the architectural tradition that has so smitten architects, artists, designers, and craftsmen and -women devoted to the elaboration of California's traditions is rooted in southern Spain.

As such, our discussions quickly shifted toward the prospects of exploring the wondrous art and ancient architectural sources that continue to inspire California architects and designers. With *The California Missions* book behind us, our respective interests soon evolved into a consideration of the role of the Andalusian tradition and its long-standing influence on early twentieth-century and contemporary California homes. As with our previous project, we wasted no time reviewing the Andalusian features and elements deemed most influential in California, not to mention the most iconic of Andalusian sites and sources that merit attention in our current treatment. In sum, our quest was on to identify some of the most iconic California homes that warranted a place in the new book. After a host of meetings with some of the most prominent contemporary architects of Southern California, it was clear that the Spanish Revival architecture of the past was finding new life in a resurgent Andalusian revival. Such considerations soon translated into Melba's travels through Andalusia in search of truly outstanding examples of the tradition. Pursuing leads brought to bear by each of our respective contacts in Spain, and, in turn, with the royal heirs and heiresses of Andalusian estates, Melba had Andalusian adventure that soon translated into a sumptuous portfolio of some of the most stunning such estates and *palacios* of the region. Among the Andalusian treasures featured here are included the fifteenth-century Palacio de Mondragón, Ronda; the late-fifteenth-century Casa de Pilatos in Sevilla; the sixteenth-century Casa Palacio de Cardenas, Écija; and the Palacio Domecq, Jerez de la Frontera, built in 1782.

Given the veritable wealth of architectural features available in this panoply of architectural expressions, we sought to extend the scope of this treatment such that we have added images from a cross section of those elements available from the great Andalusian estates or *palacios* of southern Spain. In Part One, we survey a sampling of the more iconic elements and features of the Andalusian architectural tradition of medieval Islamic Spain by way of the *palacios* of some of the leading families of the region.

(Right) Historic map of Andalusia and Granada, 1257–1479.
Courtesy David Rumsey Map Collection,
David Rumsey Map Center, Stanford Libraries

Die Iberische Halbinsel

von 1257 bis 1479.

Geographische Meilen.

Spanische Leguas.

N.B. Die historisch wichtigsten Namen sind unterstrichen.

Die Nordgränze von Cataluña.

ANDALUSIA und GRANADA.

N.B. Die beyden Nebenkarten sind im doppelten Maassstabe der Hauptkarte.

FRANKREICH — Gf. Provence — Gf. Rossillon

ASTURIEN · NAVARRA · Kr. ARAGON · Kr. CATALONIEN

CASTILIEN · LEON · Toledo oder Neu-Castilien · La Mancha

K. Cordova · K. Murcia · K. GRANADA

Mallorca · Minorca · Iviza · Cabrera · Formentera

Valencia · Saragossa · Barcelona · Madrid · Sevilla · Toledo · Granada · Malaga · Gibraltar · Ceuta

FEZ

ISCHBILIA · KORTHOBA · GRANATA · Malaka

PART ONE:

ANDALUSIAN EXPRESSIONS

(Right) Mudéjar gardens, Moorish castle walls, eleventh and twelfth centuries, Palacio Portocarrero, Palma del Río, Spain.

ELEMENTS
ARCHES CEILINGS DOORS TILES
WINDOWS FOUNTAINS

The Andalusian architectural features documented in contemporary California contexts (in the second part of the book) run the gamut from *al-Andalus* and/or Moroccan arcades and tile work to a host of exuberant *Mudéjar* water features and rock-cut courtyard fountains. Perhaps the most iconic such features that recur in contemporary California are deep-set masonry windows and doors, groin vaults, wrought-iron window grills, thickset whitewashed stucco walls, hand-hewn roofing timbers and plank doors, enclosed balconies, *zellij* tile panels, *azulejos* or glazed and colored stoneware tile surrounds, and luxuriant courtyard gardens. Interior features include coffered ceilings and tracery, ornate stone cornices and medallions, tiled cupolas and arcades, medieval wrought-iron hardware, and telescoping rectangular and circular towers. Each of these distinctive features have their origins in North Africa, Andalusia, and the Middle East. These served to bridge the traditions of the Iberian Peninsula and Andalusia from those of Morocco and North Africa by way of the Strait of Gibraltar. As the result of thousands of years of interaction via the strait, pronounced similarities in the traditions of each region coalesced around a shared cultural tradition that ultimately served to bridge the peoples and cultures of each respective region. Contemporary California, by extension, is heir to this fourteen-centuries-old tradition of opulent architecture, sophisticated artistry, and divine proportion conveyed to us through the course of centuries.

(Right) Yeseria, or carved-plaster archways, Late fifteenth century, Casa de Pilatos, Sevilla, Spain.

(*Above*) Yeseria carved plaster arches,
Casa de Pilatos, Sevilla.

(*Opposite*) Main courtyard, House of the Counts of Torres Cabrera, seventeenth
century, Palacio deViana, Ronda.

Following pages:
(*Page 32*) *Mudéjar* star vault, Baños Arabes, Ronda, Spain.
(*Page 33*) Arcade with whitewashed groin (cross) vaults, Casa Cardenas, Écija, Spain.

(Above) Yeseria arcade with multifoil arches, Patio de las
Doncellas, fourteenth century, Real Alcázar, Sevilla, Spain.

(Right) *Boveda esquifada*, Dome of the Mihrab, eighth century, Mesquita, Mosque-Cathedral of Córdoba, Spain.

(Left) Artesonado, adorned ceiling, Carmen de los Chapiteles, Granada, Spain.

(*Above*) Muqarnas, ornamented vaulting, Casa de Pilatos, Sevilla, Spain.

(*Right*) Armadura cupuliforme or dome, Salón de Embajadores, Al-Mu'tamid, eleventh century, Real Alcázar de Sevilla, Spain.

(Right) Labor de Menado wooden door,
Casa de Pilatos, Sevilla, Spain.

Following pages:
(Top left) La Alhambra, Granada, Spain.
(Bottom left) Casa de Pilatos, Sevilla, Spain.

(Right) Casa de las Dueñas,
Late fifteenth century, Sevilla, Spain.

(Page 45) Wrought iron hardware,
Palacio Peña Flor, Écija, Spain.

(Right) Zellij tile, Real Alcázar, Sevilla, Spain.

(Above) Zellij tile, and hand-carved yeseria, circa
fourteenth century, La Alhambra, Granada, Spain.

(Above) Azulejo glazed tiles, Casa de
Pilatos, Sevilla, Spain.

(*Above*) Window alcove composed of azulejo glazed tiles, Casa de Pilatos, Sevilla, Spain.

(Right) Reja, ornate wrought iron window grill,
Carmen de los Chapiteles, Granada, Spain.

Ornate wrought-iron grill or reja, Palacio Mondragón, Ronda, Spain.

Azulejos, or glazed tiles, frame this wrought-iron reja, Palacio de Viana, Ronda, Spain.

Wrought-iron window grill, Real Alcázar, Sevilla, Spain.

Wrought-iron reja with jali, or latticed screen, Palacio Mondragón, Ronda, Spain.

(*Above*) Marble fountain pedestal, Casa de Pilatos, Sevilla, Spain.

(*Right*) Marble fountain,
Palacio Domecq, Jerez de la
Frontera, Spain.

(Top) *Mudéjar* fountain, La Alhambra, Granada, Spain.

Mudéjar water channel and fountain, La Alhambra, Granada, Spain.

(Left) Marble fountain dated to 1837, Grazalema, Cádiz, Spain.

PALACIOS / ESTATES

The art and architecture of Islamic Spain, or *al-Andaluz*, flourished in the period extending from AD 711 through 1492. Thereafter, their artistic and architectural legacy endured under the *Mudéjar* artisans who remained in Iberia in the late medieval period in the wake of the Christian Reconquista of 1492. The most refined expressions of *al-Andaluz* are generally identified with the *Mezquita* or mosque of Córdoba (ca. 784–987), the fortress palace of La Alhambra (ca. 1338–1390), the adjoining palace and gardens of Generalife (ca. 1302–1324), Granada, and *La Giralda* or bell tower and former minaret of the Great Mosque of Sevilla (1184). Such palatial estates served as the cultural and political epicenters of the kingdoms and emirates of Islamic Spain. While the *alcázar* (Moorish fortress, castle, or palace) or *alcazaba* (Moorish citadel) palaces of Sevilla, Córdoba, and Granada remain the most iconic such sites, those of Ronda, Écija, and Jerez de la Frontera are resplendent with the architectural features that define the hybrid Islamic-Christian legacy of *al-Andaluz*. Invariably, the antiquity of such sites echoes several centuries of cultural, religious, and political change. The impact of such changes is reflected in the episodes of construction, deconstruction, and remodeling, as each in turn boasts the elements and features of that change borne into the present.

(Right) Fired brick pointed horseshoe arch, Palacio Mondragón, Ronda, Spain.

PALACIO DE MONDRAGÓN, RONDA

The *Palacio de Mondragón*, or *Palacio del Marqués de Villasierra*, Ronda, presents a fifteenth-century *Mudéjar-*Renaissance hybrid architectural character borne of its storied history. While the original *alcázar* is attributed to the Berber king *Abd al-Malik*, son of the sultan of Morocco, Abu al-Hasan 'Ali, the whole of the palace was subsequently occupied by the Catholic kings who conquered Ronda in 1485. The palace, rebuilt atop its original foundations, retains the architectural footprint of the first alcazar and gardens. The main gate in turn bears the heraldic crest of Captain Don Melchor de Mondragón. The *palacio* subsequently became the residence of Don Fernando de Valenzuela, the *Marqués de Villasierra*, and hence the attribution for the name of the *palacio*. The *Palacio de Mondragón* features an early sixteenth-century masonry facade, both Neoclassical and Gothic architectural embellishments and terracotta-tiled roofs, three interior patios including fountains, an ornate masonry well, arcades, a courtyard-centered cloister, *Mudéjar* doors and *artesonado* ceilings, and *azulejo* tile work throughout the whole of the complex. In 1975, the Ayuntamiento de Ronda, or Town Hall, purchased the property, and converted it to use as the *Museo Municipal de Ronda*.

(Right) Azulejo tile work graces the arcade corridor in the Palacio de Mondragón, Ronda, Spain.

Following pages:
(Left) Courtyard with fountains, Palacio de Mondragón, Ronda, Spain.

(Middle) Azulejos glazed tiles and ladrillo pavers, Palacio de Mondragón, Ronda, Spain.

(Right) Water features, fountains, and channels, Palacio de Mondragón, Ronda, Spain.

CASA DE PILATOS, SEVILLA

Construction on this renowned Italian Renaissance and Spanish *Mudéjar* palacio was begun in 1483. The construction was undertaken at a time when the late-fifteenth- and early-sixteenth-century Spanish Plateresque architectural style was in vogue. Otherwise defined in terms of a manner of workmanship akin to that of the silversmith, it consisted of an eclectic or hybrid blend of *Mudéjar*, Flamboyant Gothic, Lombard, and Tuscan Renaissance decorative elements and architectural features. Commissioned by Don Pedro Enríquez de Quiñones, IV, *adelantado mayor* or chief governor of Andalucía, and his wife, Doña Catalina de Rivera, the estate was completed by their son, Don Fadrique Enríquez de Rivera, the first Marquis of Tarifa. The palacio was erected on land seized from a Jewish family during the Spanish Inquisition. The Marquis's 1519 pilgrimage to Jerusalem so influenced him that on Lent in 1521, he officially inaugurated the Sevillian observance of the via crucis or the Holy Way of the Cross. The established route began in the *Chapel of Flagellations* of the Marquis's estate, then named the *Palacio de San Andrés*, and proceeded along a course culminating at the *Cruz del Campo*, or monumental cross, situated just outside the walls of the city. The Andalusian palace was remodeled in 1529, and the Genoese designer Don Antonio Maria Aprile then saw through the installation of the Renaissance-styled marble gateway leading into the lush gardens of the Andalusian courtyard. In 1568, the viceroy of Naples, Don Per Afán Enríquez de Ribera, commissioned Neapolitan architect Don Benvenuto Tortello to rebuild the estate, and to do so by way of preserving the original *Mudéjar* room blocks replete with their extensive floor-to-ceiling *azulejo* tiled panels and *artesonado* or "honeycomb" ceilings attributed to the artisan Don Cristobal Sanchez. To this was added an extensive collection of ancient Roman busts and Renaissance copies installed into the arches of the newly built loggias fronting the Patio Grande or garden.

(Right) The arabesque ornamentation of the carved-plaster or yeso arcades and azulejos, or tile mosaics, are a hallmark of the Casa de Pilatos.

(Left) Artesonado, adorned ceiling, carved-plaster or yeso, and azulejo tile work afford an air of opulence within the Casa de Pilatos, Sevilla.

(Left) Period paintings add to the sense of history beneath the elaborately configured artesonado ceiling of the Casa de Pilatos, Sevilla.

CASA PALACIO DE CÁRDENAS, ÉCIJA

The sixteenth century Casa Palacio de Cárdenas y Prado Castellano is one of a host of centuries-old *palacios* located throughout the ancient Andalusian settlement of Écija, in Sevilla. The Cárdenases boast a pedigree borne of early administrative and interpersonal ties to the royal court of Queen Isabella I of Castile and King Ferdinand II of Aragon, the Catholic monarchs who unified Spain with the overthrow of Muslim rule. A host of noble marriages ultimately cemented the Cárdenases's network of courtly ties as the Marquéses de La Garantía. Located astride the *Camino de Ronda* and the ancient fortress gateway, or Puerta de Sevilla, the Casa Palacio was built circa 1565 adjacent to the Torre Almohade of 1000. With a floor plan configured about a central nucleus within a walled enclosure, it boasts an eighteenth-century courtyard remodeled with modernist columns in 1897. After two hundred years as the Cárdenas estate, and with no remaining heirs, a late Baroque facade with the Martel family *escudo*, or coat of arms, was added after the property was conveyed in 1781. The living quarters running the length of the facade were subsequently converted for use as barns or stables for its internationally acclaimed Sevillano horses. With vaulted ceilings, the Casa Palacio has regal charter, yet rustic character, born of its vaunted equestrian heritage and a centuries-old identification with the *milicia real* or royal militia of Écija. The equestrian cultural heritage of Écija, and the Cárdenas family in particular, given their ties to the royal court and the Spanish military, is apparent throughout this courtly estate.

(Right) The empedrado, or pebble and cobble pavements, are a defining feature of Andalusian traditional architecture.

The groined or double barrel vault is here used to maximum effect within the porticoes (as in the stables) of the Casa Palacio de Cárdenas.

(Left) The art of esparto, or cord and grass weaving, has a seven-thousand-year pedigree in Andalusia, and graces the windows of the Casa Palacio de Cárdenas.

PALACIO DOMECQ,
JEREZ DE LA FRONTERA

The *Palacio Domecq* dates to 1782 and was commissioned by the 1st Marquis of Montana, Don Antonio Cabezas de Aranda, who ordered his palace built on the plains of San Sebastián. Located in Jerez de la Frontera, Andalusia, Spain, the estate was long identified as the Palacio del Marqués de Montana, until its acquisition by the Marqués de Domecq. This Baroque eighteenth-century estate was designed and built (over the span of several years) by Sevillian and Jerez architects Antonio Matías de Figueroa, Pedro de Cos, and Juan Díaz de la Guerra. The Marquis Don Antonio Cabezas de Aranda opted to move into the palacio prior to its completion in 1782. Only three years later, Don Antonio passed away, and upon his death, the *Cabildo de la Iglesia Colegial de Jerez* was charged with managing the Marquis's estate. The cabildo, or town hall, in turn formed a trust, which then moved to lease the palacio for reuse as an administrative building, thereby transforming the estate into the Jerez de la Frontera offices of Revenue, the Royal Customs House, and the Office of Salt. The Marqués de Montana, who died without heirs, left the estate to the cabildo, which used all proceeds to defray the expenses of the women's hospitals of the city. Some seventy years later, the former palacio of the Marquis of Montana was acquired by Don Juan Pedro Domecq Lembeye in 1855. A descendant of the storied house of Domecq de la Verguerie de Usquain of southern France, Don Juan's namesake and forebear Juan de Domecq was honored by Louis XIV, *le Roi Soleil*, the Sun King, with a pair of white gloves and a sword as an act of gratitude to him for services to the crown in 1666. From 1855 onward, the Palacio Domecq became the epicenter of a family dynasty renowned for the Domecq label of fine wines and brandies based in Jerez de la Frontera.

(Right) Like the *riads* of Morocco and Andalusia,
such enclosed patios or gardens trace their ancient
pedigree to North Africa and the Middle East.

(Top) Wrought-iron window grills, chandeliers, tapestries, and an armadura *Mudéjar* or coffered ceiling lend to the dignified air of this stairwell.

(Left) The magisterial proportions of this stately dining area are accented by chandelier, armadura *Mudéjar* or coffered ceiling, and Andalusian studded plank doors.

(Top) The armadura *Mudéjar* and hand-carved plank doors lend to the regal character of this residential corridor.

(Left) An armadura *Mudéjar*, ornate colonnade, and marble flooring front a courtyard within the Palacio Domecq.

(Right) The three-tiered Palacio Domecq retains much of its original character in the form of arcades, coffered ceilings, patios and courtyards, and intricately crafted details.

PART TWO:
SPANISH STYLE HOMES
IN CALIFORNIA

(Right) Christiancy Estate, architect Lillian Rice,
1927, Rancho Santa Fe, California.

The Ruskin

Architect: Frank Meline, Scott Lander

Build: 1922, Remodel 2014

Location: Los Angeles, California

Rescued from oblivion by a visionary designer, Scott Lander of Lander Design, this 1922 Mission Revival-style residence was first built to serve the needs of the nearby Congregational Church Extension Society. Originally designed by noted local architect Frank Meline to serve as a Sunday school room and parish house, the Methodist Church soon conveyed the property to the celebrated Ruskin Art Club for use as a clubhouse in 1926. As one of the oldest and most storied such clubs in Los Angeles, the Ruskin Art Club has long served as a center for the promotion of the arts and culture of Southern California through a calendar of social and cultural events and performances by new and established artists, arts scholarships, and community activism. In so doing, the women of the Ruskin Art Club facilitated the establishment of some of the leading arts and cultural organizations of the Los Angeles Basin, and did so by way of extolling the virtues of art critic John Ruskin's social activism, and thereby, its namesake's vision for the "unity of life and art." A product of the Arts and Crafts movement of the late nineteenth century, the club was founded as such as a women's group by Mary E. Boyce in 1888, and remains one of the "most influential cultural and arts associations in the Southland." The Ruskin Clubhouse was the home of this juggernaut of artistic and cultural production and community pride.

(Right) The spacious meeting room of the former Ruskin Art Club was reborn at the hands of designer Scott Lander.

For nearly ninety years, the Ruskin was the epicenter of the Ruskin Art Club or salon and its yearly calendar of programs and events devoted to featuring the works and performances of both established and emerging artists. In 2014, with the economic realities that the club was facing, and mounting costs to maintain a clubhouse in dire need of rehabilitation, the club sold the compound to designer Scott Lander, who promptly moved on the renovations needed. Lander Design has transformed the former parish house and Sunday school into one of the premier homes of Los Angeles, and he did so in record time. Such was the pace of Lander's commitment to the rehabilitation and restoration that local residents of the Windsor Village Historic District, in which the former clubhouse is situated, initially protested the conversion of the former parish property. Moreover, the building's status as Historic-Cultural Monument No. 639 of the City of Los Angeles only served to heighten tensions.

Despite those community concerns initially raised, Lander Design's conscientious and deliberative approach to honoring the Ruskin's historic status was paramount, and that while in the throes of renovating a complex of buildings clearly in dire need of rehabilitation. Though the interiors were construed a wreck, Lander determined that the "bones of the building" were good, and the building was therefore deemed worthy of being brought back to its former glory. In order to achieve the renovation, it was necessary to strip extant wall and ceiling treatments and floor coverings, and replace them with interior treatments needed to complement and enhance the Mission or Spanish Colonial Revival character of the original 1920s-era residence. To that end, Scott Lander preserved the most iconic elements of the interior spaces while adding upgrades throughout the three-bedroom, two-and-a-half bath estate and guesthouse. As such, the design plan included refurbishing such features as the original Batchelder tile fireplace, the open-beam

(Left) The interplay of wooden lintels and door and window surrounds lends to the appeal of this 1920s-era estate.

ceilings, and the grouping of French doors opening onto an idyllic Mission Revival style–central courtyard with a fountain. Enclosed on all sides by room blocks and tiled arcades, the generous proportions of the courtyard and its drought-tolerant plantings lend to the open and inviting character of the residential compound.

As to the success of Lander's reenvisioned single-family residence, borne as it were from the bones of a historically significant Mission Revival style–building, in 2014 *Curbed* identified the Ruskin as one of the "Most Beautiful Houses for Sale in 2014." Their assessment was based on its "excellent decor, riveting architecture, or something hard to define that we'll just go ahead and call 'soul.'" Moreover, the Los Angeles City Council has repeatedly passed resolutions acknowledging the fact that where the Ruskin Art Club and its membership is concerned, "There is hardly an established cultural institution in Los Angeles to which Ruskin Art Club members have not made landmark contributions."

(Above) The exterior elevations belie the influence of the Spanish California missions, particularly insofar as the bell wall and arcades are concerned.

(Right) The interior courtyard is lined with olive trees and a fountain, and it speaks to the Mediterranean influences of an earlier time.

Casa Andalusia

Architect: Maurice Swetland

Build: 1926

Location: Altadena, California

Casa Andalusia was conceived and designed by New York writer and publisher Maurice Swetland, an executive of the United Publishers Corporation, publishers of *American Architect*. Drawing on a family history of foreign travels throughout Europe, Swetland was particularly inspired by the Andalusian tradition of southern Spain, and this in turn prompted him to bring together the most iconic features of Andalusia and the *Mudéjar* into the design of his personal residence. Built in 1926, Casa Andalusia embodies the mystique and aura of the Southern California penchant for Spanish Revival style–residential architecture at its best. With an asymmetrical floor plan replete with terracotta-tiled roofs punctuated by *ladrillo*-tiled courtyards, multiple patios and three hornos or fireplace features, masonry arches and post-and-lintel arcades, enclosed wooden balconies, colorfully tiled steps, and a loggia, the home is a visual delight and exemplar of the 1920s Spanish Revivals of the time.

(Right) Casa Andalusia features many of the design sources of the Mission and Spanish Revivals in vogue at the time of its construction in the 1920s.

Situated in the shadow of the Mount Wilson Observatory on the southern flanks of the Angeles National Forest near Eaton Canyon Falls, Casa Andalusia remains a veritable oasis on the margins of the urban sprawl that defines the Los Angeles Basin.

Drawing on the mixed sensibilities of the architectural treatments of the 1920s, both the interior and exterior features and landscapes constitute a panoply of Andalusian, Moroccan, Spanish Revival, Southwest Pueblo, and Mexican design elements and features. Terracotta tiles, whitewashed stucco walls, colorful Andalusian and Mexican tile work, wrought iron window grills, and the *Mudéjar* relief of the door surround all add to the allure of the estate.

(Above) High walls, tiled fountains, and nichos, or alcoves, for the saints all come together in this portion of the estate.

(Right) The principal elevation speaks to the *Mudéjar* stylistic traditions of Spanish Andalusia.

Where the interior treatments are concerned, these are many and varied, and run the gamut from vintage to contemporary. Andalusian stylistic elements are reflected in its Moroccan lamps, sconces, mullioned windows, hardwood and Saltillo-tiled floors, beamed cathedral ceilings, Talavera-tiled fountains, and masonry niches. Elaborately crafted wrought-iron banisters, grills or rejas, chandeliers and wooden window screens further emulate those of southern Spain. Tiled wall, floor, bath, and door and window surrounds are to be found throughout, and further lend to the charm of this estate. French doors and a dining area that extend into an adjoining den and loggia add to the open

(Left) Beamed ceilings of rough-cut timber vigas complement terracotta-tiled floors, wrought iron, and azulejos, or tiled risers, in this elaborately designed stairway.

and inviting, and timeless atmosphere of Casa Andalusia.

Enveloped in a canopy of oak trees, and boasting Valencia oranges, a grapevine-covered arbor, and walkways crafted from sandstone pavers, the home's interiors seamlessly open into a lush tapestry of both native and introduced plantings and manicured lawns. The award-winning gardens and the temperate

(Top left) The renovation of the interior features of Casa Andalusia lend to its air of refinement.

(Bottom left) The beamed ceilings, wooden columns and ornate metalwork spans conjure the Mashrabi-ya, or projecting oriel windows and wooden lattice panels of Andalusia.

(Top right) Tile features and molded surrounds enhance the bar and dining areas.

(Left) Ladrillo-tile flooring and turquoise paint lend to the inviting atmosphere of Casa Andalusia.

(Above) The enclosed patio beckons the visitor to enjoy the serenity of this Andalusian-styled space.

(Following pages) The two-story elevation fronting the courtyard patio incorporates an enclosed second floor portico fashioned after those of the Mashrabiya or projecting window screens of Andalusia.

climate conjure the exoticism of southern Spain and its cultural landscapes, while the low masonry compound or perimeter wall lends itself to the sense that one has entered into an exclusive and otherworldly time and place. In the final analysis, the elaborate hardscape and mature landscape features that envelop the property lend a heightened sense of antiquity and authenticity identified with the residence and its Andalusian pedigree.

Casa Blanca

Architects: George Washington Smith, Henry Lenny

Build: 1927, Remodel: 1996

Location: Carpinteria, California

In 1927, renowned Santa Barbara architect George Washington Smith designed and built the Moroccan-inspired Isham natatorium or pool house for then owner Albert Isham's Casa Blanca Sandyland beach complex in what was then known as Sandyland. The beautifully tiled interiors and Moorish wainscot of the spacious and exotic Moroccan pool house features a tiled mural inspired by Persian miniatures. Moreover, the whole of the building includes magnificently decorated Islamic pointed and horseshoe archways with tiled surrounds and a sun roof, or trough ceiling, framed in the finest of *Mudéjar* woodcraft tracery. In effect, George Washington Smith's original design plan was based on that of a Moroccan mosque replete with flat roofs, minaret, dome, scalloped walls, and *Mudéjar* arches. Whereas the exterior of the building features stark white and scalloped stucco walls, domes, and tiled courtyards, the Moroccan pool-house interior is an oasis of color, charm, and serenity.

Enter architect Henry Lenny of the Henry Lenny Design Studio and his team. An accomplished architect and former commissioner to the Santa Barbara Historic Landmarks Commission trained at the Universidad Autónoma de Guadalajara, Mexico, Lenny's portfolio spans some thirty-

(Right) The opulent and refined Casa Blanca, with its zellij-like tiled fountain, evokes the ambience of the coastal African nation of Morocco.

five years of inspired and visionary architectural creations from throughout Southern California. In this instance, the architect and homeowner affected the design plan for the 1997 build of the Casa Blanca estate. The Casa Blanca is an oceanfront property situated on a point with majestic views of the Pacific Ocean on three sides, and the Los Padres National Forest to the north. The Isham natatorium, or pool house, designed and built by George Washington Smith constitutes a central feature of the opulent cluster of contemporary Moroccan-styled estates identified with the former Sandyland beach complex.

Ideally suited to the temperate, Mediterranean-like, climate of Southern California and the California Riviera and Coast Ranges, the Moroccan-styled residence boasts a broad array of Andalusian and North African architectural features and decorative elements. The unmistakable Andalusian flair and Moroccan character of the whole of this lavish complex speaks volumes to the rich tapestry of details that went into the design of this oceanfront property. In effect, the ambience is palpable both within and without the whole of the

(Right) The refined look of the living room arrangement is highlighted by the majestic oculus window.

estate, and upon approaching the main entryway, one is left to ponder the North African sensibilities of the place, replete with palms, *zelij*-like tiled fountains and water features, terracotta tile drives, stark white walls, domes, and arches. The interiors of the Casa Blanca are a visual delight of Andalusian and Moroccan windows and doorways, wrought iron railings, archways, and coffered ceilings, and are in effect a testament to the merits of a remodeling effort that spans the period from 2013 through 2019.

(Above) The arabesque lines of the niches and alcoves of the Casa Blanca are enhanced with the placement of fine glasswares.

(*Left*) The solarium remains a popular feature of the Moroccan *riad*, or guesthouse, centered on an enclosed garden.

(*Above*) Window in the form of a classic Andalusian pointed horseshoe arch.

(Above) The wondrous symmetry of the
Andalusian tradition is borne of the balance of
geometry and the use of light.

(Right) The coffered ceilings of Andalusia are
here echoed in their reincarnation in masonry,
lathe, and plaster, as opposed to wood.

(Left) The Moroccan pool was designed to integrate the opulence of a bygone era.

(Above) Renowned Southern California architect George Washington Smith designed this iconic pool, or hammam. It remains the sole vestige of the complex for which it was originally built.

Mendelsohn Residence

Architect: Percy Parke Lewis

Build: 1927, Remodels: 2004, 2017

Location: Los Angeles, California

A mere three years prior to his design and build of the famed Spanish Mission Revival–styled Fox Westwood Village Theatre, architect Percy Parke Lewis was granted a building permit for the Mendelsohn Residence of 1927. In 1931, the Fox theater in Westwood Village was opened to considerable fanfare and significant accolades for its Spanish Mission Revival plan replete with Churrigueresque stucco design elements, and an iconic 170-foot-tall gleaming white tower. The tower immediately captured the public imagination in what was then deemed the Spanish Revival/Moderne style of the day. In that same year, the Mendelsohn Residence was completed, and bore many of the hallmarks and much of the charm of any of the opulent Spanish Mission or Colonial Revival–style estates located in the heart of Los Angeles. Situated just west of the margins of the Los Angeles Country Club, this was the place to alight with the Hollywood set. With all of the trappings of Andalusia and southern Spain, the estate opened to the stately serenity and tranquility often conjured by the art and architecture of the al-*Andaluz*. While Percy's residential creation has matured into a sanctuary and retreat from the hustle and bustle of the big city, the Fox theater, by contrast, remains the dynamic centerpiece for a nearly ninety-year run of major motion picture premiers, Hollywood elite, and the indomitable paparazzi of the day. Film and television producer Carol has since found

(Right) The Mendelsohn Residence maintains lush gardens and stately fountains as well as Andalusian and early California design motifs.

sanctuary in this Spanish Colonial Revival residential masterpiece, with its elegant array of Andalusian details that evoke the nostalgia and charm of old Hollywood. With credits ranging from her signal contributions as indefatigable co-creator and long running Producer of such famed network television shows as *CSI: Crime Scene Investigation, CSI: Miami, CSI: NY, and CSI: Cyber*, Mendelsohn would be the first to acknowledge that where her home is concerned, "it's my retreat from life in the city, where I take time for myself." As with much of the Andalusian tradition, the atmospheric qualities of the interior opens into a vibrant urban oasis of plants and water features that embody the serenity and qualities that she seeks in her home.

The Mendelsohn Residence was the subject of major remodels or renovations in 1931, and again in 2003 and 2004. Whereas the previous homeowners, Geoff Grisham and Robert Rischer, undertook a major remodel just prior to the acquisition of the residence by the current owners, the hardscape and exterior plantings that speak to the design plan of today are the vision of April Palmer Landscape Design, who oversaw the landscape enhancements of 2015–17. And much to her credit, the landscape design of the Mendelsohn Residence clearly conforms to Palmer's view that such landscapes are rendered into "a three-dimensional art form, a dynamic, evolving canvas in which the element of time interplays with form and space." Accordingly, Southern California's climate provides an ideal setting for the seamless flow of indoor-outdoor living. To that end, colorful Moroccan tile wall and tiered masonry fountains were installed in varied settings. These range from those wall fountains located astride the full-sized swimming pool and second-story outdoor patio with fireplace to that of the tiered fountain and Mudéjar basin that anchors the backyard hardscape. The loggia, or partially enclosed patio, fronting the backyard in turn features a Spanish Colonial–style fireplace and *Mudéjar* star window within a beautifully appointed outdoor space.

As for the sumptuous elegance of the interior design, and its storied furnishings and art works, those were brought into the light through the combined efforts of Carrie Hauman Designs, and Sally Hendrickson Fine Art & Treasures.

(Right) With citrus trees, palms, and a variety of ornamentals, the stately gardens of this Los Angeles home conjure the Mediterranean lifestyle.

With a thematic range spanning women in the West to Andalusian splendors, the decor is clearly inspired. In effect, the home's varied, albeit pleasantly subtle color scheme, is paired with colorful and evocative art, Moroccan tile, lamps, and interior window grills. Its embellishment is achieved with contemporary rugs and multiple fireplace features. The home's *Mudéjar*-style stuccoed vaulting and beamed ceilings lend much to that level of serenity found to reside here in the Mendelsohn Residence. As Carol says, "my living room is the first...I truly 'live' in. I read, write, sing and dance, meditate, entertain friends. And, it's the perfect place to take a nap." In effect, it is imbued with the "balance, serenity, spirit, soul, heart and tranquility" sought by her design team.

(Left) Southwest-inspired art, and Oriental and Andalusian traditions all coalesce in the collections that grace this home.

Following page:
(*Top left*) Featuring beamed ceilings, hardwood flooring, and Mudéjar windows and archways, the Mendelsohn Residence exudes charm and refinement.

(*Bottom left*) The kitchen evokes modernity though the lens of a bygone era.

(Right) An otherwise simple staircase is complemented by the placement of a *Mudéjar* window and wrought-iron grill.

Opposite page:

(Top left) The warmth of the Southwest color palette
envelops the bedrooms, hallways, and living areas
of this home.

(Middle left) Cowgirls and the open range of the West
dominate the themes selected to define this living area.

(Bottom left) The archways, hardwood floors, and muted
tones of this passageway contrast with the exuberance of
the artwork installed at this location.

(Left) The Spanish style hearth feature comes replete with
azulejo tiled risers and surround, and painting of
a Southwest cattle drive.

(Above) The exoticism of the tile work and Moroccan color
palette of the bathroom generate a soothing ambience.

(Opposite) The veranda features a
Spanish-style fireplace
with azulejo surround.

(Below) The *Mudéjar* geometry of this wrought-
iron window feature is akin to those that once
graced many a California mission.

(Left) The refined geometry of the water feature and its azulejo tiled decor recalls the *Mudéjar* windows fronting the pool.

(Right) The rooftop solarium features an intricately tiled fountain.

Casa Colibri

Architect: Cameron Crockett

Build: 1928, Remodel: 2011

Location: Long Beach, California

Situated just over a block from Ocean Avenue in Long Beach, California, Casa Colibri, constructed in 1928, bears many of the hallmarks of the Andalusian tradition. Borne of the efforts of the current owners' desire to highlight and enhance the Spanish style, the home has experienced a rebirth at the hands of Hollywood set designer Adrianna Lopez and architect Cameron Crockett. As homeowner, Lopez, and her husband, Paul Olson, have worked to remodel their home such that they have enhanced the Andalusian features and integrated Spanish Revival elements that once dominated the area in the 1920s and '30s. So as to extend the warm and inviting ambience of the original home into the surrounding landscape, Adrianna recruited landscape architect Jim O'Neill, who in turn recommended architect Cameron Crockett. The trio has captured the essence of Andalusia through those remodeling efforts completed in 2011.

Situated in the Belmont Shores neighborhood, Casa Colibri was built at a time when the Spanish or Andalusian style was in vogue throughout the Alamitos Peninsula, and it was then that the nearby Seaside Walk Boardwalk was installed near the pier. The popularity of the area has long drawn many noted celebrities, including Upton Sinclair, the author of *The Jungle*, who used one of the peninsula's summer homes as a

(Right) The white facade, terracotta-tiled roof, and *Mudéjar* door and window features of Casa Colibri conjure the elegant simplicity of the Andalusian style.

writing retreat. Sinclair is said to have had a host of notable summer visitors, including internationally renowned physicist Albert Einstein, and actor and comedian Charlie Chaplin. The Spanish Revival style predominated, thereby transforming Belmont Shore into a haven for summer visitors and those seeking a respite from the hustle and bustle of the big city.

The Andalusian sensibilities of the home were enhanced through the deliberative efforts of the homeowners to instill the residence with Moroccan or North African features and elements, not the least of which include the "Blue Wall." Distinctive in its design and placement, the Blue Wall partitions the rooftop deck from the adjoining terracotta-tiled rooftop. With an undulating Spanish *espadaña* or bell gable form, and seven niches and two wrought-iron lamps, the Blue Wall enhances the privacy and generates a sense of serenity for the rooftop refuge so prized by Adrianna and Paul. At the same time, the now beautifully weathered bell-gable feature evokes the rich hues and exoticism of Moroccan blue, used in roof and floor tiles, atop domes, and across the exterior walls of homes and civic buildings in Fez, Morocco. According to Adrianna, the rooftop deck and Blue Wall are central to what she and Paul most enjoy about the tranquility and peace conjured at Casa Colibri. At the same time, the rooftop deck permits a modicum of relaxation enhanced by the sounds of beachgoers enjoying the beauty of the temperate and inviting California coast.

Given the Andalusian propensity for placing a premium on residential interiors that open onto exterior courtyards and landscapes, both Adrianna and Paul sought to introduce the same into their home without significantly modifying the original plan. As such, Casa Colibri's landscape features extend the ambience of the interiors into exterior spaces. In addition to the tiled terracotta roofs, whitewashed walls, archways, and beam-studded ceilings of the original dwelling, Casa Colibri now boasts a plush landscape, Andalusian-style tiled walls and floors, and a beautifully crafted wrought-

(Right) Archways, elaborately tiled floors, and fine woods complete the ensemble fronting the living room.

iron spiral staircase extending from the kitchen to the rooftop deck that opens to the heavens. A particularly unique feature of the residence is that centered on the walkable skylight that partitions the rooftop deck from the lush "jungle-like" plantings of the bathroom below. With Andalusian and Moroccan design considerations deemed central to the design, Adrianna sought to integrate a range of California native plants both within and without the house. These have, in turn, lured hummingbirds to the residence in such numbers that the owners' were inspired to name the residence Casa Colibri, after the Spanish term for hummingbird.

(Top left) The simple charm of the kitchen and dining areas speak to the California lifestyle.

(Bottom left) The beamed ceilings of the living room recall the massive timber work of the California and Southwest missions.

(Right) The stairwell leading to the rooftop solarium is lined with an ornamental metal railing that lends to the elegance of the passage.

(*Left*) The bath and relaxation rooms of Casa Colibri were designed to create a contemplative atmosphere.

(*Above*) The bath feature is intricately tiled from floor to ceiling.

(*Following pages*) The turquoise-colored rooftop solarium wall remains a central feature of this Moroccan design vision.

Aimino-Boone Residence

Architect: Gilbert Stanley Underwood, Designer: Mark Boone

Build: 1928, Remodel 2018

Location: Los Angeles, California

Rarely does one find a family home built as the personal residence of a renowned architect of the golden age of Hollywood, and that replete with its intact suite of Spanish Revival–era design elements and features. Nestled in the Hollywood Knolls area of Los Angeles and in the shadow of the celebrated "Hollywood" sign overlooking the Los Angeles Basin, famed architect Gilbert Stanley Underwood found refuge at this crossroads of the film industry, lying as it does between Universal Studios, Warner Brothers, and the Hollywood Bowl. One year prior to building his dream home in the Hollywood Knolls in 1928, Underwood established himself as an architect and designer of the indomitable and iconic Ahwahnee Hotel situated in the Yosemite Valley with views of Half Dome, Glacier Point, and Yosemite Falls. In short, Underwood distinguished himself as the prolific architect and designer of National Park Service lodges and Union Pacific depots across the country. His project undertakings span Zion Lodge in Zion National Park, Bryce Canyon lodge, the San Francisco Mint, the Post Office Annex in downtown Los Angeles, and federal courthouses in Seattle and Los Angeles, with a signal contribution to his role as co-designer of the State Department building in Washington, DC.

(Right) The Spanish Revival was central to architect Gilbert Stanley Underwood's efforts to create a place called home.

(Above) The unassuming character of the main elevation contrasts sharply with the renown of its creater, architect Gilbert Stanley Underwood.

The comfortable charm that this vintage home affords is attested to by the fact that both its architect and designer, Gilbert Stanley Underwood and his family, and a subsequent family, were long-lived residents of this Spanish Colonial Revival residence. In fact, prior to the recent acquisition of the property by Mark Boone and Dennis Aimino in 2017, the last residents were comfortably ensconced in the residence for some fifty-six years.

Enter interior designer Mark Boone, the principal of Mark Boone, Inc., Interiors, and the 1920s-era Spanish Colonial Revival residence soon underwent the makings of a transformation, but one respectful of the preservation of authentic infrastructure and the interior finishes and treatments of the original home. According to Mark Boone, "a careful, multi-year plan is in place to restore and refurbish the home to its original stature as an important example of Spanish Revival architecture by a celebrated architect." Accordingly, Mark acknowledges that the

(Above) The integration of a repeating series of pointed arches recalls the use of the multifoil arch in the fourteenth-century churches of Andalusia.

(Above) Moroccan ornamental lamps, both lanterns and chandeliers, conjure the exotic.

"good bones are still there," but the process will entail "peeling back layers and restoring neglect" in order to reveal the original spirit of this Spanish Revival masterwork. Worthy of the planned makeover, Mark intends to preserve the warm, intimate, and romantic characteristics of this venerable Spanish Andalusian, and Southern Californian, estate. To do so, such details as wrought-iron and other period fixtures and hardware, beam studded ceilings, weathered pocket doors, exposed wooden headers, wide-plank flooring, a veranda, and a wood-burning fireplace, are all aspects of the original build plan to remain uppermost in those considerations underlying the projected remodel.

Among those features that both distinguish the residence, and curry Mark's favor are those central to the Andalusian design tradition. These include the respective proportions of the rooms, Andalusian arches and original pocket doors opening onto the courtyard and other public areas, cantilevered architectural elements, beautiful detailing throughout, and a private walled courtyard replete with an original

fountain. Of course, it does not hurt that the whole of the parcel has views of the Hollywood Hills and Pacific coastal range, with sunsets deemed nothing less than spectacular. Mark makes clear that the property remains a "hidden jewel of a neighborhood which loops around the Hollywood Reservoir," thereby affording "great hiking, wildlife, and peace in the heart of the chaos of Hollywood."

(Left) Though Gothic in origin, Bay windows have their counterpart in the *Mudéjar* mashrabiya, or lattice enclosed projecting oriel window or screen.

(Above) Masonry walls and wooden gates evoke the enclosed gardens central to the *riads* or courtyards of Morocco.

(Right) Timber colonnades and terracotta-tiled roofs and walkways front the enclosed courtyards of many a Spanish Revival residence in California.

Smithson-Steinway Residence

Designer: Ann Pirhonen

Build: 1928, Remodel: 2007

Location: Los Angeles, California

Renowned Los Angeles area visual artist and photographer Aline Smithson and husband Henry Steinway first purchased this 1928 Los Angeles property in 1996. According to Aline, "I always wanted to live in a Spanish style house"...like those out of the glory days of Hollywood. This penchant for capturing the spirit of old Hollywood and the Andalusian Revival era in her home setting is reflected front and center in her biography. Her bio unflinchingly asserts that Aline is "best known for her conceptual portraiture and a practice that uses humor and pathos to explore the performative potential of photography. Growing up in the shadow of Hollywood, her work is influenced by the elevated unreal." And it is, in fact, the "elevated unreal" that defines the design ethos and objects that she spirited into the decor, design, and details of her Los Angeles–area home.

In 2007, this Spanish Colonial Revival estate was given a major makeover with the addition of a second story. Staying true to the design characteristics of the original 1928 residence, Smithson and Steinway elaborated and expanded upon the existing Andalusian and Spanish Colonial Revival features of the home. Drawing on those design details

(Right) A bougainvillea envelops an Andalusian-styled fountain replete with brass fixtures and azulejo glazed tiles.

already present on the first floor of the 1928 plan, Aline recruited designer Ann Pirhonen, and the two worked closely on the design plan for a second floor addition. In effect, the objective was to "replicate the downstairs plan upstairs...and therefore, details from the first floor and fireplace were mirrored on the second floor."

Ultimately, Aline revealed that the design plan and remodel were inspired by the photography of Melba Levick, whose previous Rizzoli books, including *Casa California*, were instrumental inspirations for the remodel and second story addition to this 1928 estate. Where the hardscape and water features of the home are concerned, Aline further acknowledged, "I was influenced by a fountain that I'd seen in another of Melba Levick's books...so, as you can imagine, when I learned that our house would be featured in the current book, we were quite excited."

Having contracted with Corner Construction for the design-build of the remodel, Aline was instrumental in this yearlong labor of love, and to that end selected all tile, lighting, and decor. In fact, Aline worked diligently to find vintage fixtures and tile, with upstairs tile matched to the era, including the Hispano-Moresque type identified with Malibu tile, first

introduced to California and US consumers at San Diego's Panama-California Exposition of 1915. According to Aline, "the house has elements that nod to chinoiserie, so in terms of decor, I tried to blend my love of mid-century chinoiserie, and Spanish influences." When asked about the peacock standing atop the bannister, Aline noted, "I love taxidermy. We have a fawn and deer as well, and each speaks to my love of things that are not real, inanimate, or should I say, not alive."

As to the results, Aline loves her home and the many details introduced into the remodel. She would as such be the first to say that she achieved the objective of transforming this Spanish Revival residence into a "House of Laughter," a house filled with light and spirit. This she attributes to the fact that "there's a happiness there! Some of that comes from the sense of whimsy, humor, and the absurd" that went into the decor. Having grown up in Los Angeles, Aline has always maintained a "love of old Hollywood." In fact, in the "living room there are two massive portraits of Charlton Heston. Why Heston? I went to a club for comedians in Beverly Hills, a famous nightclub, and they were having a garage sale...and I bought the Heston portraits there, and they have been in my living room ever since." Although

(Left) Mediterranean lines and Andalusian features coalesce in the design of the Smithson-Steinway residence.

she maintains that she has no connection to Heston: "I grew up in an environment where everything had to do with the movies, and therefore I developed a fascination with stage sets...thereby making the unreal seem real."

(*Right*) Azulejo glazed tiles frame the Andalusian hearth under the watchful gaze of Charlton Heston.

(*Below*) Nineteenth-century portraits, wrought iron, and a peacock ala taxidermy grace this stairwell within the Smithson-Steinway Residence.

(Left) Beamed ceilings and stylized archways cojure their Andalusian inspirations.

(Right) Original elements of the Andalusian Revival of the late 1920s are preserved in several interior spaces.

(Left) Period lighting features remain to illuminate Andalusian Revival era hand painted ceiling embellishments.

(Right) A mix of modern furnishings, *Mudéjar* archways, and timbered ceilings complement the Andalusian fireplace of this interior space.

Camina con Cristo

Architect/Designer: Thomas Callaway

Build 1928, Remodel 2007

Location: Los Angeles, California

Residential designer Thomas Callaway is an artist and visionary of many talents, a Renaissance man in every sense. Thomas, or Tom Callaway, began his career as an A-list Hollywood actor, and as life would have it, some of the biggest names on the Hollywood scene lured him into the world of interior design. Tom has starred in such network television productions as *Murder, She Wrote, Murphy Brown, L.A. Law,* and *Designing Women*. His signature roles include his portrayal of Colonel James W. Fannin in *The Alamo: Thirteen Days to Glory*, and as Texas Joe Grant in *Young Guns*. Tom nevertheless retired from the world of acting in 1995 to pursue his newfound passion in interior design.

In a 2019 interview for *California Home+Design*, Tom revealed how his passion for residential design was brought to life through his years as an A-list actor. According to Tom, "I create an imaginary story for every project, i.e., how it came to be, etc., and then design to make the story become real life." In this way, Tom's vision is to script the story behind his creations, and these span a broad range of production roles and design types, including residential design, planning and construction, landscape design and interior decoration. As with those actors who go on to direct film and television, Tom has taken to supervising both the design and build of his

(Right) The spacious grounds of this 1920s-era Spanish Colonial and Mission Revival estate remain central to designer Tom Callaway's vision for a family-friendly environment.

respective "stories" such that he has often worked tirelessly and meticulously to assure that the stories are fully and authentically revealed through his creations. To that end, it's not uncommon for Tom to remain on site for long hours so as to oversee the completion of specific design concepts and details. In one such instance, Tom hovered over the completion of a stone and stucco wall and hand-adzed wooden beams to assure that they resonated with the "right feel" for the Spanish Colonial Revival style he sought in that instance.

As with the A-list residential design preferences of 1920s and '30s Hollywood, Tom is best known for his expertise in the medium of Spanish Colonial and Mission Revival, and his creations make clear the desire to infuse each of his creations with an air of authenticity. For Tom, his proudest work is that of this opulent Spanish Colonial compound that he designed in Los Angeles, and named Camina con Cristo. In this instance,

(Above) Violet wisteria grace the arcade fronting the manicured grounds.

(Right) Beamed ceilings, wrought-iron, an inviting fireplace, and *Majolica* earthenware ceramics draw on their Spanish Colonial and Mission Revival inspirations.

his clients sought to transform their 1928 Brentwood Park residence into an estate worthy of grand family gatherings. In so doing, Tom rose to the challenge through a project that spanned three key stages of development that entailed a wholesale remodel of the main estate, and the construction of new ancillary features, including a New Mexico–style Mission Revival or folk chapel, between 1998 and 2007. As Tom says, "of the 200 or more projects in my design career, this project, and its completeness of style, detail, and multiple structures, stands above the rest in the satisfaction of meeting my highest goals."

Invariably, both Tom and his clients have acknowledged that their favorite feature remains the Mission Revival chapel at the heart of the compound. In executing this new build, Tom recruited noted decorative painter Esther Carpenter, who drew upon Mission-era artworks and wainscoting selected by Tom to see through a wealth of stenciled wall decorations throughout the chapel and residential remodel. All stenciled and hand-painted *vigas*, or hand adzed roof beams, door surrounds, wainscoting, and walls were completed by Esther. Moreover, Esther transformed the chapel's centerpiece into

(Opposite) The Andalusian-inspired fireplace feature and Alfarje-like beamed ceilings lend to an air of antiquity.

(Top left) Alfarje-inspired horizontal wood beamed ceilings grace these interiors.

(Bottom left) The Camina con Cristo residence integrates christian icons and artworks *throughout.*

(Right) Beamed ceilings, eighteenth-century portraits, wrought-iron railings, and azulejo-tiled risers all lend to the dignified character of this stairway.

a richly painted New Mexican–styled altarpiece, complete with period liturgical pieces selected by Tom. Esther's fellow Mississippian, Garth Benton, entered the fray for two years to see through the paint scheme identified with the so-called Tower, or second floor landing replete with clearstory windows and classically inspired paintings. Benton, whose work graces the Getty Villa in Malibu, was instrumental to seeing through the Spanish Colonial Revival style identified with the paintings that grace the second-floor landing in particular.

Not to be outdone, a recent article from *The Most Expensive Homes* rated Thomas Callaway one of the "Most Incredible Top 20 Interior Designers from L. A." Given how it was that Tom entered the field of interior design, from the rarified atmosphere of the A-list Hollywood scene, it is clear that Thomas Callaway has cemented his place among the top residential designers of southern California. In so doing, he continues to tout Camina con Cristo as his proudest achievement. This surely speaks to the authenticity, brilliance; elegance, intimacy, and nostalgia that Tom sought to inflect into this most opulent of Brentwood Park estates. For the owners, Tom's efforts have been rewarded by

(Above) The beamed and gabled roof and Andalusian-styled fireplace of this room are particularly reminiscent of the salas, or living areas, of the California missions.

their acknowledgement that his creation has engendered "a wonderful and special place in the owner's hearts." In the final analysis, Tom is particularly proud of the family and social life that his proudest achievement has taken on in the ten or so years since the wholesale remodel and build that produced Camina con Cristo.

(Left) The tower, or second-floor landing, was embellished with classically inspired liturgical murals.

(Right) Gabled roofing, weathered-plank wood doors, and wrought-iron hardware lend to the ambience of virtually every room of Camina con Cristo.

(Above) Camina con Cristo has been
redesigned to reflect the needs of family
and community.

(*Above*) This timber-and-masonry loggia provides the ideal setting for retreats and family gatherings.

(Opposite) Designer Tom Callaway is particularly proud of his efforts to see through the addition of this Spanish Mission-styled chapel.

(Right) The interiors of the chapel were inspired by the Franciscan mission churches of New Mexico.

La Habra Heights

Architect: Robert Sinclair

Build: 1929, Remodel: 1935, 2001

Location: La Habra Heights, California

The community within which the La Habra Heights residence is located lies in a pass just south of the San Gabriel Mountains. La Habra, or "pass through the hills," was named by the Spanish commander Gaspar de Portolá y Rovira (1723–1786) and Friar Junípero Serra, OFM (1713–1784), during the course of the Sacred Expedition of 1769. This momentous venture culminated in the settlement of Monterey and the exploration of the San Francisco Bay. La Habra was as such the gateway to upper or Alta California, and the founding of the Spanish settlements of Northern California. This Spanish Colonial Revival estate celebrates in planning, decor, art, and furnishings, this early foray into the enchanted and storied world of early California history and tradition.

Built on the eve of the Great Depression that began in October 1929, this Andalusian-styled estate was effectively completed in 1935. Despite proving to be one of the most opulent of the palatial estates of that time, further enhancements were undertaken in that year, thereby setting the standard that would endure through the remodel and addition of recent years.

(Right) The Andalusian architectural traditions of southern Spain are well suited to the celebrated Mediterranean climate of coastal California.

Enter celebrated Southern California architect Robert Sinclair of Sinclair Associates Architects, Inc., and his team in 2000. For this project, Sinclair joined forces with interior designer Matthew White of White Webb, LLC, and landscape architect Katherine Spitz of Katherine Spitz Associates, Inc. Together, they saw through an addition and the wholesale renovation of this historic residential estate and gardens on a parcel spanning six acres. White brought to the table the inspiration of his many years studying an array of historical styles and cultures, and a rich tapestry of arts and architectural traditions. Named to the *Architectural Digest* list of the one hundred best designers in the world, his influence is seen in the opulence and authenticity of the *al-Andaluz* and North African sources for the interior design of the La Habra Heights residence. The richly textured historical traditions of the design standard brought to bear permeate the atmosphere of this storied estate. At the same time, elements of the Spanish missions era are found distributed throughout the residence, including images of California missions founding father Friar Junípero Serra, OFM, and the Spanish explorers,

saints, and luminaries of the eighteenth century and beyond. Landscape architect Katherine Spitz in turn oversaw the design plan for both the plantings and hardscapes of the estate. With palm trees, olives, and crimson bougainvillea gracing the grounds, Katherine's eye for the early California and Mediterranean worlds permit one to

experience that time and those places in such a fashion as to unite the opulence of the residential interiors with environmentally compatible plantings in the outdoor setting.

With over a dozen terracotta-tiled gabled or pitched-roof features, white-stuccoe walls, and cylindrical towers on a horseshoe-

(Above) Beamed ceilings. wrought-iron banisters and chandeliers, and azulejo glazed tile risers complete this Andalusian ensemble.

(Right) The circular tower that dominates the La Habra Heights residence draws on the inspirations of the Andalusian armadura *Mudéjar*, or spoked ceiling in this instance.

shaped plan, the La Habra Heights estate reveals the very best of the Andalusian tradition. The asymmetrical floor plan as such is a defining feature of the residential plans of southern Spain and North Africa. The magnificent tower situated immediately adjacent the main entryway to the residence heralds the transcendence of the place, and evokes the atmosphere and sensibilities of another time. Upon entering the La Habra Heights residence, one is immediately struck by the warmth, charm, and majesty of the interior appointments and architectural treatments. With an eye for the interplay of light and shadow in his creations, architect Robert Sinclair generates spaces that conjure the "light, darkness, balance, movement, tranquility, and continuity" of a given time and place.

Sinclair's studied eye for the merits and artistry of *al-Andaluz* in particular have been brought to the fore in this tribute to the art and architecture of southern Spain. His love for historic architecture and his many forays into those regions that drive his passion and vision have clearly influenced his architectural creations. Vaulted or open gabled ceilings with Andalusian *vigas*, or girders, solid-core wooden doors, wrought-iron railings and lamps, *zellij*-styled Moroccan-tile stairway risers, flooring, and walls all hearken to the Moorish and Spanish Revival styles of 1920s Southern California and beyond. In the final analysis, the spoked or ribbed wooden ceiling, or *artesonado*, of the tower, and rooms embellished from floor to ceiling with Andalusian tilework speak volumes of the tradition of craftsmanship that first gave birth to this sprawling estate.

(Left) The beamed and gabled superstructure, with iron straps and clavos, or nails, draws from the architecture of the California missions.

(Top) Bougainvillea graces the archway leading to a water feature.

(Bottom) Porticoes and loggias remain an enduring feature of Andalusian architecture and its inspired expression in California and the Southwest US.

(Right) As with the finest of Andalusian palacios and estates, water and lush gardens conjure the sacred landscapes of southern Spain.

(Following pages) The verrière, or glass enclosed sun parlor, affords a respite for reading and relaxation.

Desert House

Designer: Doug Smith

Build: 1945

Location: Palm Springs, California

In the 1920s, the population of Palm Springs scarcely surpassed some two hundred souls, yet today, it has a thriving populace of some 47,000. Touted for its secluded resort-worthy location and hot, dry, sunny desert climate, Hollywood notables, including internationally renowned writers and artists were drawn to build retreats in Palm Springs. This pattern originated and only intensified with the area's reputation for health-related tourism, famed mineral springs, and the buildout of a series of luxurious resort hotels, casinos, and golf courses. The Oasis Hotel (1925), the Renaissance-styled El Mirador hotel, and the Palm Springs Tennis Club (1927). The Hotel del Tahquitz (1929) and O'Donnell and El Mirador golf courses launched the makings of the desert resort's fame as a desired destination. Such was the growing popularity of Palm Springs in the 1920s that a host of A-list celebrities and social elites were drawn to build homes and estates in the Warm Sands, the Mesa, and Historic Tennis Club neighborhoods that comprise the western margins of the city.

The Mesa neighborhood within which the Desert House was built has its origins as a gated community of the 1920s. Dubbed the Hollywood Hills of Palm Springs for its eclectic architecture and relative privacy, the idyllic neighborhood has, and continues to lure the Hollywood set and its cast of characters. Its most notable residents both past and present include King Gillette, Zane Grey, Clark Gable,

(Right) Moroccan furnishings and whitewashed walls of this Palm Springs residence conjure North Africa and *al-Andaluz*.

Carole Lombard, Suzanne Somers, Herman Wouk, Henry Fernandez, Barry Manilow and Trina Turk.

A grant deed dated to 1932, and cement block construction materials, provisionally date Desert House to 1945. Constructed at the height of the war, and in the wake of General George S. Patton's use of the region as a training ground for the European campaigns of WWII, this Spanish Revival–style residence retains its Andalusian features and oasis-like qualities and charm. Situated near Indian Canyons, the house was built at the height of the mid-century modern craze that swept California and the West in the period extending from 1933 through 1965. This was a period of architectural experimentation that came to encompass a range of mid-century modern designs, and given the Spanish Revival Style of the Desert House, it's a wonder that the design remained true to the spirit of Andalusia. Even so, today it continues to be characterized as both Spanish and Hacienda in design.

With spectacular views of the San Jacinto Mountains to the west, and first- and second-story bedrooms bathed in the dawn's early light of the east, Desert House evokes the architectural traditions of Morocco, Andalusia, and Southern California in one fell swoop. The host of updates and modern amenities introduced by designer Doug Smith effectively complement the home's classic contours. Boasting terracotta-tiled roofs and flooring, sun-drenched white-washed walls, weathered French doors, pitched beam ceilings, palm trees, wrought-iron gates, and wooden arbors, Desert House conjures the heyday and romance of California's Spanish Colonial and Mission Revival glory days. Even so, the incomparable tranquility of the Moroccan compound encircling the shimmering blue pool and distant palm trees is enough to seduce even the most stoic of hearts.

(Left) The Mediterranean climate of Southern California is ideally suited to xerophytic or drought-tolerant plantings.

Following pages:
(Top) The massive handcrafted doors, archways, and whitewashed walls of this study undoubtedly inspire creativity.

(Middle and bottom) Open gabled ceilings afford a sense of spaciousness to this single story Palm Springs bungalow.

(Right) This Andalusian inspired hearth speaks to the warmth and charm of this Palm Springs home.

Kovalik
Residence

Architect: Jeff Shelton

Build: 1951, Remodels: 2000, 2005

Location: Santa Barbara, California

The creations of architect Jeff Shelton are anything but your standard fare, and in fact any review of Jeff's work will evoke a range of classically and not so classically inspired artists, architects, and designers. A 2015 feature article by the *Los Angeles Times* cited Jeff in characterizing his work as "asymmetrically symmetrical—and a bit over the top." What with Spanish architect Antoni Gaudí, Dutch graphic artist M. C. Escher, and American author and illustrator Dr. Seuss cited by media sources as presumed inspirations for his most public buildings, is it any wonder that those seeking the whimsical flair of Catalan modernism turn to Jeff Shelton?

Unlike the vast majority of Andalusian expressions in Southern California, Shelton's designs conjure the admixture of *al-Andaluz*, Catalan, and Mediterranean, architectural styles. The Kovalik Residence is ideally suited to the temperate Mediterranean-like climate that drew the early Franciscan friars to the region. In this instance, the 1951 residence has undergone multiple remodels and renovations, including those of 2000 and 2005, with Jeff Shelton's work representing the latest iteration of the transformative process that produced a home filled with light, color, and otherwise whimsical Gaudí-like design features and decorative elements.

(Right) An Andalusian-inspired fireplace with embedded azulejo tiles is framed within an alcove fronting the living room.

The Kovalik Residence is nestled in the Santa Ynez Mountains along what has been deemed by many the "American Riviera" for a geography and climate that approximates that of the northern Mediterranean Sea coast spanning the shores of Spain and France, and the French Riviera. From its ornate wrought iron second- and third-story balconies, one can gaze on the expanse of the seemingly limitless Pacific Ocean and Coast Ranges, and thereby take a moment to bask in the California sun and revel in the sights and sounds of this idyllic community with the lure of the distant surf. With a host of panoramic vistas, wrought iron balconies, whitewashed stucco, asymmetrical floor plans, terracotta roof and floor tiles, glazed door surrounds, colorful exterior canopies, and both gabled and hipped roof types, the Kovalik Residence is no less than a visual delight. The open, bright, and charming character of the overall design scheme is continued into the interior plan such that exterior tilework is mirrored on the interiors, along with a panoply of whimsical wrought iron architectural details, metal lamps, Andalusian arches, and inviting fireplace features.

(Above) Wrought-iron hangers and a green and white-tiled kitchen area evoke the country homes of Andalusia.

(Above) Glazed tiles frame this entryway in a manner reminiscent the zellij hand cut tiles of North Africa and *al-Andaluz*.

(Right) The terracotta tiles, wrought-iron window grills, and tiled entryways are here counterbalanced by the Gaudí-like plate-iron gateway.

Holmby Hills

Architect: Robert Sinclair

Build: 2001

Location: Los Angeles, California

This majestic 12,925-square-foot residential estate and gardens is a masterful blend of Tuscan villa opulence and the Andalusian Revival style built in 2001. With a mandate to design and build an Italian Tuscan villa–like estate, architect Robert Sinclair was challenged to integrate those elements of the Andalusian style most befitting the early twentieth-century estates of old Hollywood and Beverly Hills. According to Sinclair, "My client base all reference these old Hollywood estates, and many were influenced by Melba Levick's books." He in turn cites those inspirational forms borne of church architecture, because, as Sinclair notes, "churches were created to move you like no other type of architecture. Particularly as many focus on volume, and on the darkness looking into the light, where light is consciousness."

With owners Jack and Joelle Rimokh affording the builders and designers a wide berth in so far as resources to achieve the refined details to be found throughout, Sinclair achieved that "European sense of warmth and intimacy" sought by the owners. In order to effect the majestic scale and textured richness inherent in the Holmby Hills estate, Sinclair drew on the very best of materials, such as authentic or historically appropriate stone for the construction of arches, groin

(Right) This Holmby Hills estate evokes the finest of both Tuscan and Andalusian craftsmanship and character.

vaults, flooring, and fireplaces. To this was added a panoply of old or "natural" woods for the hand-hewn roofing beams and flooring, original or historic bricks for walls and bridgeways, boulders for waterfalls, and other natural materials for the splendid fountains that grace the grounds.

In order to bring their vision into the light, Sinclair and his team, including interior designer Mark Boone of London Boone, Inc., sought to assure the opulence and atmospheric qualities of this Beverly Hills estate. Even so, the owners were instrumental in furnishing the estate in a fashion befitting their lifestyles, while at the same time mirroring the majesty of the estate and its surroundings. Landscape architect Robert E. Truskowski in

Previous pages:
(Left) Florida Keystone was used throughout the estate to achieve the refined appearance featured.

(Right) Groin vaults and classically inspired columns define the colonnades of the Holmby Hills estate.

(Above) The masterful deployment of groin vaults and rock-cut fireplace features draws on the medieval charter underlying both the Andalusian and Tuscan architectural traditions.

Following pages:
(Top left) Wrought iron balustrades and lanterns, groin vaults, and shimmering marble floors enhance the opulence of this estate.

(Bottom left) Finely crafted wrought-iron gateways and fireplace features lend an air of refinement to the estate.

(Right) Skylights and an oculus define the interplay of light and shadow in an atrium-like setting overlooking the foyer.

turn assured that the grounds were of a quality that evoked the Mediterranean Basin in every way, including such plantings as mature olive trees culled by purchase from other communities of the Los Angeles Basin. To this collection were added crimson bougainvillea, exceptionally tall junipers, ivy-covered walls, palms, and a host of perennial plants and tiled driveways.

The mature landscape plantings in effect evoke an antiquity and age seldom experienced in modern estates, and an anticipation and reverence of place is borne of the lengthy tiled drive that wends its way through a tree-lined pathway to the forecourt of the estate.

Whereas the main facade of Holmby Hills constitutes a blend of Tuscan and Andalusian elements, the interiors bespeak a Mediterranean elegance and sophistication unanticipated from the outset. The blend of exterior features, including stuccoed elevations, asymmetrical roof and floor plans, archways, brick vaulting, towers, arcades, colonnaded loggias, weathered brickwork, groin vaults, climbing vines, tiled corridors, enclosed balconies, iron grillwork, terracotta tiled roofs and pavers, all speak to the Andalusian character of the estate. The interiors, by contrast, constitute an architectural masterpiece of alternating brick, masonry, and Keystone groin vaults, arched doorways and corridors, ivory stuccoed walls, hand-hewn *vigas*, or exposed roofing beams, stone colonnades, Tuscan (stone) fireplaces, niches, wood-framed skylights, wrought-iron balustrades and door and window grills, terracotta-tiled flooring, and rock mosaics.

Of those features noted, Sinclair is particularly proud of the exceptional quality and elegance of the limestone groin vaults fabricated from only the finest of Florida Keystone, a material identified with such qualities as aesthetic appeal, durability, and appearance. The mastery of the work lends itself to a subtle mood that defines the very charm and character of this Holmby Hills estate. As one of his first commissions, Sinclair acknowledges that the estate brought together the eclecticism and character of a Tuscan villa with a suite of Andalusian elements intended to play on those ethereal qualities of light and shadow that define the architectural ethos that Sinclair brings to bear in all of his project undertakings. To that end, Sinclair says, "all of my designs are courtyard-based, bringing together the dimensions of negative space such that all rooms and interiors flow into the courtyards, thereby providing a cooling effect on the atmospheric qualities of the building."

(Left) The wondrous craftsmanship of Tuscan stonework is found throughout the estate.

(Above) The integration of antiquarian features
and mature landscape plantings was meant to
engender a sense of tranquility.

Trousdale Estates

Architect: Marc Appleton

Build: 2004

Location: Beverly Hills, California

Nestled in the foothills of the picturesque Santa Monica Mountains of the Pacific Coastal Ranges of California, Trousdale Estates has long drawn public figures, including civic leaders, Hollywood celebrities, and the elite and moneyed families of California. Its community pedigree includes entertainers Groucho Marx, Elvis Presley, Frank Sinatra, Dean Martin, Ray Charles, Tony Curtis, Jennifer Aniston, David Spade, Jane Fonda, and former president Richard Nixon, among others. Heir to the creative talents of such world-renowned architects as Frank Lloyd Wright (1867–1959), Paul R. Williams (1894–1980), Wallace Neff (1895–1982), and A. Quincy Jones (1913–1979), this Beverly Hills community is a veritable barometer of the eclectic architectural expressions rendered by California architects and designers over the course of the past sixty-five years.

Enter world-class California architect Marc Appleton of Appleton Partners LLP, whose byline is one borne of "an enterprise of quiet but attentive craft." Renowned as one of the premier Spanish Colonial Revival specialists of California, his creative contributions to the genre are nevertheless many and varied. Whereas the client for the Beverly Hills estate in this instance originally sought to

(Right) Tapestries and a wrought-iron balustrade and wall sconces highlight the opulence of this spiral staircase.

have a Mediterranean-style home built for housing a first-rate collection of early twentieth-century plein-air paintings and Mission-style furnishings, Appleton soon convinced his client that the Spanish Colonial Revival style would best suit the traditional dimensions of the Southern California scene. With that in mind, the 1920s-era designs of noted architect George Washington Smith soon took the day. So it was that Appleton and his team were off and running on the design and build of a truly opulent estate grounded in the arts, history, and traditions of Southern California.

(Above) Evocative of the courtyard gardens of Andalusia, this forecourt offers respite from the workaday world beyond.

Drawing on the long-lived mystique of Andalusian and early California design features that define the architectural traditions of some of the most noteworthy estates of Southern California, Appleton sought to generate an aura of opulence borne of historical pedigree. To assure their shared vision, Appleton recruited the interior design team of Mark Enos and Carmen Reese of Enos Reese + Co. Devoted to architectural integrity and the inventive use of historical and cross-cultural motifs, the interior design team achieved its goal, and one that shines true in the interior decor of this Trousdale Estates residence in particular. Where hardscape design and plantings are concerned, Sean Knibb of Knibb Design saw through a luxurious and atmospheric landscape that complements the setting with introductions true to the designer's aspirations for integrating elements of fantasy, drama, and creature comfort.

(Below) The architectural lines, including cylindrical tower feature, and terracotta-tiled gabled roofing hearkens to the palacios of Andalusia.

Featured in the October 2006 issue of *Architectural Digest*, this estate was the product of a concerted effort by the architect to address the owner's desire for a measure of "monastic elegance" grounded in tradition. A critical source of inspiration in this instance was that brought to bear through the residential designs of the legendary architect George Washington Smith, and Appleton's desire to create a one-of-a-kind estate. In the final analysis, the sparkling interchange between the design team and the client was dutifully distilled—and faithfully executed, to achieve the desired results. The resulting George Washington Smith–inspired Spanish Colonial Revival estate comes with both authentic and faithfully reproduced Andalusian furnishings by the interior design team of Enos Reese+Co, and a hardscape with courtyards, loggias, and a pavilion. The mature heritage landscape that complements the estate was brought to fruition by landscape designer Sean Knibb's introduction of hundred-year-old olive trees from Northern California, an apropos design feature truly herculean, albeit appropriate, by its very nature.

(Left) The spiral stairway framed by the cylindrical tower is delineated by a masterfully crafted colonnade.

(Above) Both charm and opulence are manifest in the furnishing of the many rooms of the estate.

(Above) Beamed ceilings, plank flooring, and
uncoursed rubble masonry kindle the charm of a
country kitchen.

(Above) The masterful craftsmanship of this space, and its coffered ceiling, is reminiscent of that gracing the many palacios of Andalusia.

(Above) The Tuscan elegance and Andalusian enchantments of a thousand years seemingly coalesce in these stately spaces.

(Left) The towering palms
that frame the view of this
wonderfully tiled loggia evoke
the Moroccan skyline.

Bel Air Crest

Architect: Robert Sinclair

Build: 2006

Location: Los Angeles, California

This sprawling 15,578-square-foot Andalusian Revival–style estate is situated atop a prominent ridge overlooking the Los Angeles basin. The sumptuous architecture brought to bear at Bel Air Crest hearkens to the ancient Andalusian traditions that gave birth to the opulence and richly textured dimensions that renowned architect Robert Sinclair seeks to infuse into all of his most spectacular designs and builds. The grandiose qualities of this wondrous estate were reified by Sinclair's stated mandate to introduce light in ways that enhance both a sense of intimacy and well-being. For Sinclair, Bel Air Crest is truly palatial, "a house like an Andalusian palace." In this instance, "light breaks up the house in interesting ways, with light piercing the darkness, and accentuating both volumes and curves that define movement through space ... thereby producing a threefold character, with expanse defining intimacy, and light and darkness generating a sense of well-being."

In order to bring to fruition this Andalusian vision, Sinclair was inspired by the owner, whose father was a prominent architect in Spain. She, in effect, introduced the architect, now renowned for his Andalusian designs, to the traditions of *al-Andaluz*. The grand sense of place, where one transits through an archway into a courtyard, and onward through a massive wood-plank door and wrought iron gateway

(Right) The wondrously designed and manicured landscapes were inspired by the Islamic gardens of Andalusia, with charbagh, or the quadrilateral garden layouts and water features of the Alhambra.

192

ultimately drew Sinclair's interest in the traditions of southern Spain. The whole of the estate, including all landscape features and mature plantings, was brought to bear from the once-barren grounds at the summit of the hills that gave rise to Bel Air Crest. While Sinclair and the owner advanced the modernized vision of an opulent palatial estate with some of the most notable Andalusian features of southern Spain, landscape Architect Greg Grisamore of Greg Grisamore Design, Inc., created a luxurious landscape clearly inspired by the Islamic palace gardens of the Alhambra in Granada, Spain. The exquisitely designed gardens of Bel Air Crest were inspired by the sacred geometry of the palacios of southern Spain, containing such features as the *charbagh* or *chahar bagh*, a quadrilateral garden layout identified with the paradise of Islam and the four gardens and water features of the Quran.

(Above) Beautifully configured groined or cross vaults, and classical Greco-Roman busts and fireplace are here fused with the mystique of the modern.

(Right) A Byzantine biforium, or ajimez (double-arched), window beautifully pairs with the adjacent monumental gateway replete with wrought-iron reja, or gate.

The asymmetrical roof and floor plans, terracotta-tiled roofs, arcades, courtyards and arabesque loggias; masonry water features; and three sizable square and circular skylights all lend themselves to the spacious yet intimate, exotic yet inviting, and intricate yet soulful, subtle, and comfortable qualities of this Sinclair creation. Inspired by the whitewashed villages of Andalusia in southern Spain, Sinclair drew on his studies of the historic traditions of *al-Andaluz* to create the white stucco exteriors of a residential complex intended to appear as though it was born of the earth, in a fashion both naturally organic and mathematically geometric. With arcades, gateways, gardens, and negative space interspersed throughout, Bel Air Crest reflects the best of the Andalusian tradition both within and without the footprint of the main residence.

According to Sinclair, a favorite feature of the Bel Air Crest lies with the brilliant and masterful stonemasonry reflected in the multitude of groin vaults, arches, and fireplace features by interior designer Dimitri Agraphiotis of Compass. To his credit, the sophisticated design of the interior arcades and limestone vaults and fireplace features is owed to Dimitri's vision for the geometry of the homes interior treatments. The Byzantine windows, while unanticipated, are entirely appropriate to the eclecticism of *al-Andaluz* and its artisans. The undulating limestone vaults that grace the arcade corridors, reception areas, and individual rooms throughout the estate speak to the artistry of Dimitri's masterful facility with masonry, as well as Sinclair's use of light and shadow such that light plays off the vaults and generates a sense of movement, majesty, and Gothic intrigue.

(Left) The groin or cross vaults of this arcade corridor amplify the depth and monumentality of the Bel Air Crest estate.

The interplay of light and shadow reflected from marble flooring with inset mosaics is echoed in the timbered *artesonado* ceilings comprised of several woods, placed to generate patterns echoing the design of the marble floors. Solid-plank doors and wrought-iron hardware and chandeliers throughout lend to that sense of history and artistry borne of the *Mudéjar* artisans of medieval Spain. The spiral staircase with gracefully executed wrought-iron railing in turn conjures a tapestry of light and shadow such that one is drawn to such amenities as the timbered and painted arabesque loggia overlooking the Los Angeles Basin. Each volume of space within this palatial estate resonates with the antiquity, opulence, and sacred geometry of another time, while at the same time affording that modicum of modernity required to enhance the charm and essential intimacy needed to make one's home.

(Above) The loggia-like character and manifold archways of this dining area presents a most inviting aspect.

(Right) A rill, or axial water channel, culminates in a quadrilateral garden or charbagh.

(Following pages) An ogre-like figure forms the hearth of this courtly patio arrangement, and seemingly invokes the spine-tingling tales of the forests of Andalusia.

La Casa Amada

Architect: Kevin A. Clark

Build: 2007

Location: Santa Monica, California

Architect Kevin Clark seeks a creative balance between the practical considerations of everyday life and the places and settings within which he designs every new build. A key consideration in all designs that evoke the Spanish Colonial Revival styles of the early twentieth century strive for the simplicity and romance of the era that produced the California tradition. Kevin thereby seeks a "natural progression of the great work done in this style in the 1920s." Therefore, it was to that end that La Casa Amada was designed for a client enamored with the vibes of the world of music, and all that the Southland has to offer in the way of access to aficionados and practitioners, producers and players.

Situated just east of the Channel Islands and within a ten-minute drive of the Getty Villa, La Casa Amada, or the Beloved House, is the product of a shared vision between world-class architect Kevin Clark and his clients. With majestic ocean views on the one hand, and the twilight of the city lights on the other, La Casa Amada presents an intriguing juxtaposition of elegant simplicity and a refined sense of place and history. While the street-side views of this Spanish Colonial Revival afford the unassuming character of a modest terracotta-tiled and cross-gabled Spanish-style residence, it clearly offers much more than meets the eye for casual passersby.

(Right) The sheer simplicity of design, and unassuming character of the main facade, nevertheless conjures the mystique of *al-Andaluz*.

Whereas mature olive trees and a luxurious hedge form a natural barrier to a full-on view of the front yard and the main facade of the residence, the asymmetrical plan, terracotta-tiled roofline, and whitewashed stucco walls speak to the historicist architectural origins of this charming home. Upon entering this Spanish-style single-family residence, one is immediately drawn into what is clearly a sizable estate spanning two floors, and appointed with hardwood and tiled flooring, wrought-iron embellishments, railings and chandeliers, and a beautifully tiled fireplace. The open rafters of the gabled living room, replete with arched doorways and massive plank doors and Moroccan-tiled stairway risers all hint to a tranquil and monastic-like atmosphere. The host of windows dominating the two-story south elevation in turn afford views of Will Rogers State Beach and the distant lights of Long Beach and Catalina Island. The stairway landing fronts a window composed of a masonry lattice that selectively permits the passage of light in a fashion reminiscent of the star windows of the Alhambra in Granada, Spain.

(Opposite) The Andalusian hearth ,with hand-painted designs that evoke the zellij tile work of Morocco and Andalusia, pairs well with the beamed and gabled ceiling elements.

(Left) A reja, or wrought-iron balustrade is paired with colorful azulejo glazed-tile risers.

(Following pages) The bamboo-shrouded brick patio affords sweeping views of thePacific Ocean.

El Sueño

Architect: Kevin A. Clark

Build: 2008

Location: Santa Monica, California

When aficionados of the Andalusian style and Spanish Revival design come together, the results are invariably nothing less than spectacular. And, so it was that when Los Angeles entrepreneur Michael Rosenfeld was drawn to the work of renowned architect Kevin A. Clark, Rosenfeld had no hesitation asserting from the outset: "You design it, and I'll build it." To that end, Rosenfeld recruited Clark and interior designer Madeline Stuart based on another outstanding project collaboration by Clark and Stuart for musician Lindsey Buckingham. That project resulted in the design and build of an Andalusian-inflected residence in Bel Air. Such was the mantra under which Clark completed the transformation of a vacant parcel of land into one of the premier estates of the region. Situated on a one-acre parcel fronting a eucalyptus-shaded fairway, El Sueño is described by the architect as a four-year courtship with the owner's vision for the buildout of a truly majestic Spanish Colonial Revival home. Completed in 2008, El Sueño is the product of a labor of love and an ongoing collaboration between the owner/entrepreneur, architect, and interior designer. In this instance, the owner blessed the project with the kind of autonomy and resources rarely seen in such monumental undertakings.

(Right) A lavishly tiled rill fountain with a linear water feature forms the nucleus of the forecourt of the El Sueño estate.

As a bibliophile for any and all books and materials concerned with the Andalusian traditions of southern Spain, not to mention the Mission and Spanish Colonial Revival styles of California and the West, Clark is a master of the medium. Moreover, he is a connoisseur, master artisan, and architect of the sublime. His reverence for Andalusian architectural expressions and Spanish Colonial revivals is manifest in his admiration for the great works of the architects George Washington Smith and Wallace Neff, among a host of others who have afforded him inspiration. For Clark, the golden age of California architecture crystallized in the 1920s, when Andalusian and Spanish Colonial revivals were a hallmark of the period, particularly for Hollywood celebrities, and the image-makers of the day. Having once owned a home designed and built by George Washington Smith, Clark seeks to integrate the sense of authenticity and the intimate and warm qualities of the Spanish Colonial Revival styles of that time.

As to how Clark articulated both his and his client's love for the Andalusian expressions brought to bear in the golden age of California's love affair with both Mission and Spanish Colonial revivals, these are evident throughout the residence dubbed El Sueño (the Dream). Amazingly, the approximately 20,000-square-foot

(Left) The foyer is dominated by a marble recreation of the star motif of the Il Redentore church of Venice, Italy, designed by Andrea Palladio.

(*Above*) Gothic, medieval, and North African influences all coalesce in this room, and within the Andalusian style more generally.

residence exudes an intimacy borne of the interplay of light and shadow. As Clark explains, "I have a passionate interest in creating formal public rooms that gave way to a relationship to the exterior spaces and courtyards," thereby creating a home that would be forever inviting to its owners. In order to assert the effect of an Andalusian estate, while preserving the intimacy and warmth often lost in the fortress-like Spanish Colonial Revival homes of the early twentieth century, Clark worked the light such that he introduced as much light as possible into the interior spaces of this abode. Moreover, despite the barren patch of land upon which El Sueño was erected, Clark designed a luxurious landscape borne of the import of mature trees and shrubs. The landscape features

were in turn complemented by exterior balconies of turned wood and wrought iron, and an iconic tiled *Mudéjar* fountain inspired by that of the Alhambra in Andalusia. As with the home's enchanted exterior features, interior amenities spare no expense, and range from the installation of such architectural embellishments as an entryway featuring a marble floor inspired by the star motif of the Il Redentore church of Venice, Italy, to period furnishings and classical works of art.

(Above) The coffered ceilings and archways of this luxurious sitting room speak to both the serenity and opulence of the estate.

(Right) The elaborately crafted armadura, or coffered ceiling, and Andalusian hearth harmonize well with the Solomonic or helical columns that gracefull meld with the powder-blue interior of this opulent space.

(Left) The rill, or linear water feature, and the adjoining Andalusian pebble pavements partition lush landscape of El Sueño.

(Right) El Sueño is ideally suited to the Mediterranean climate of Southern California.

(Following pages) The spillway of the eight-pointed star fountain, with its azulejo glazed-tile embellishments, feeds the adjoining rill.

Del Mar Beach House

Architect: Marc Appleton

Build: 2009

Location: Del Mar, California

The Del Mar Beach House represents the very best of recent designs centered on the Spanish Colonial Revival styles of California and the West. The evocative and historic character of such homes was the inspiration of a generation of architects lured to Andalusia in the golden years of a phenomenal style that spanned the 1920s and '30s in Hollywood and the Southland. With architects George Washington Smith and Wallace Neff at the helm of the Spanish Colonial Revival and Andalusian Revival movements of the time, Hollywood and the California Riviera were transformed to the extent that city ordinances were enacted to sustain the style in perpetuity. As such, contemporary architects continue to find inspiration in a style rooted in Andalusia and the Spanish, Moorish, Mission, and Mediterranean revivals of the early twentieth century.

One such devotee of the Spanish Colonial Revival style, and one of the leading architects of the era, is renowned Southland architect Marc Appleton of Appleton Partners, LLP. Marc established his practice in the heart of the Spanish Revival style capital of California, Santa Barbara. It was there in 1976 that Marc founded his firm with a reputation rooted in drawing on the architectural traditions and historic features of many a bygone era. Since that time, he and his associates have designed some seven hundred

(Right) The wonderful symmetry of Del Mar Beach House overlooks and contrasts with the vastness of the Pacific Ocean.

projects for both public and private clients, including residential, commercial, and institutional builds. Marc eschews calls to brand a signature or singular style, and instead works across a broad range of materials and media, historical contexts, and architectural styles. With a portfolio construed as both diverse and eclectic in its range, Appleton Partners readily acknowledges a vision for an "enterprise of quiet but attentive craft." This ethos drives Marc and his team, and has done so to the extent that they have garnered a host of *Architectural Digest* awards for being one of the top hundred designers in the world.

Built in 2009, the Del Mar property is exceptionally intimate, quiet and attentive to traditional Andalusian details in virtually every sense of the word. With majestic ocean views, stark-white stucco walls, and both terracotta roof and floor tiles, a courtyard with outdoor pool, and *Mudéjar* water features, Del Mar Beach House is ideally suited to finding sanctuary in the shadows of the workaday world and the hustle and bustle of the big city. Situated just north of San Diego, the locale affords the best of all words, both terrestrial and marine.

This inviting, and seemingly unassuming, abode is richly attired in the treasures of Andalusian artistry. Interiors feature arabesque wrought-iron gates and Moroccan lamps, a seemingly ancient breezeway festooned with *zellij*, or Islamic tile, mosaics, colorful wainscot patterns,and hand-hewn open *viga* ceilings, and each exudes an inborn sense of intimacy and tranquility. Upon entering the interior of the Del Mar residence, the exuberance of the *zellij* tile mosaics, wainscoting, and door surrounds reinforces the arabesque, and the finest of such works from southern Spain. Wrought-iron and Moroccan metal lamps grace the breezeway and interiors, and afford a warmth and feeling of ease not often found in modern buildings. Whether seeking solace in the family

(Above) Roses grace the archways and exteriors of the terracotta-tiled Del Mar Beach House.

sitting area, or rest and relaxation in the expansive great room or outdoor courtyard, the refined character and unassuming opulence of Del Mar Beach House is the stuff of memories and many a moment of contemplation.

(Above left) Wrought-iron gates, or rejas, and lanterns are here juxtaposed against the Andalusian-styled pebble pavements of the forecourt.

(Above right) This groin- or cross-vaulted zaguan passageway emulates the zellij-cut tile mosaics of many an Andalusian palacio.

(Above) Azulejo glazed-tile archway surrounds and wainscoting lend an air of exoticism to the design of this coastal California estate.

(Left) Beamed ceilings, alcoves, and an Andalusian hearth engender a stately sense of place.

(Above) Azulejo glazed-tile doorway surrounds complement the lapis lazuli blues of the shower stalls, and terracotta-tiled flooring.

(Right) The masterful tile work of the bathroom was clearly inspired by the arts of Andalusia.

(Above) A wrought-iron *reja*, or banister, partitions the distinctive geometry of the stairwell.

(Left) The Andalusian, Moroccan, and Spanish Colonial Revival furnishings and chandelier of the gabled bedroom offer a dignified and serene refuge from the world beyond.

El Andaluz

Architect: Jeff Shelton

Build: 2009

Location: Santa Barbara, California

World-renowned Spanish architect Antoni Gaudí would have been proud to make the acquaintance of architect and designer Jeff Shelton, with his whimsical eye for an architecture of the surreal. El Andaluz represents a labor of love by Jeff and his team of artisans and craftspeople. Described as a visionary architect and artisan who turned Spanish Revival architecture on its head in Santa Barbara, the flamboyance, bold forms, and vibrant colors of each of his award-winning projects has spawned a walking tour that encompasses some ten of his most notable works. Dubbed the "Jeff Shelton Architecture Walking Tour," the tour provides a self-guided contemporary option to Santa Barbara's traditional Red Tile Walking Tour of historic buildings and landmarks. Situated in the heart of downtown's farmers market, with both luxury shopping and a selection of upscale and reasonably priced restaurants, El Andaluz affords a host of modern amenities and majestic views of the Santa Ynez Mountains and the California Riviera.

(Right) The resplendent and eccentrically atmospheric qualities of the work of renowned architect Jeff Shelton are on full display in El Andaluz.

El Andaluz was built up from a parking lot razed for new construction in 2009. In a *Design Bureau* 2012 feature article and interview with Jeff, the architect says "We turned our construction site into an art studio, full of artisans who wanted to put their talent into the building." The eclecticism of the team clearly translated into the artistry and design details of the whole of this upscale Southern California condo complex. An extraordinary range of design motifs, materials, methods, and talent went into the elaboration of the whimsical ambience of this Santa Barbara masterpiece. Ornamental ironwork, including one-inch thick galvanized-steel loggias found throughout the complex, are unique for both the material type, application, and contexts within which they were used. Both the loggias, and the exuberantly tiled courtyard with its exotic fruiting trees, are among Jeff's favorites at El Andaluz. The liberal use of geometrically diverse and colorful tile patterns, wrought-iron railings, galvanized steel loggias, and richly carved woods speak to the extraordinary character of a building that has been likened to Antoni Gaudí's famed Casa Batlló, or House of Bones, in Barcelona, Spain. While the style and de-

(*Left*) The turquoise and terracotta color palette, horseshoe archways, and water features of the courtyard conjure the enchantments of *al-Andaluz*.

sign plan of El Andaluz has been characterized by its architect as Spanish Revival Sheltonesque, it clearly lives and breathes the spirit and collective visions of Gaudí, Salvador Dalí, and M. C. Escher.

The ground-floor arcade and walkway of the main facade of El Andaluz was boldly inspired by the Andalusian architectural masterwork, the *Mezquita*, the Mosque-Cathedral of Córdoba which melds the sacred worlds of both al-Andaluz geometry and color with the Iberian tradition of cathedral building. Whereas the enclosed wooden balconies and *viga* ceilings of Andalusia have here been replaced by blue-gray galvanized custom steel loggias and whimsically detailed rafters, the elaborately crafted *artesonado* wood ceilings replete with a decorative geometric patterning pay tribute to the *Mudéjar* traditions of southern Spain. And, as with the great Moorish *palacios* or Alcázar of Andalusia, the interplay of light and shadow, interior courtyards and ornately tiled water features, and exotic plantings all bespeak an otherworldly engagement with the peoples and places of the *al-Andaluz*.

(Right) Drawing on the inspiration of the renowned Catalan architect Antoni Gaudí of Barcelona, David Shelton Design fashioned these balconies from one-inch-thick galvanized steel.

(Above and left) The mashrabiya or enclosed oriel window or screen-like room block situated above the main entryway to the complex evokes the folk art of Andalusia.

(Opposite page) David Shelton's ironwork designs grace the whole of the complex, and lend to the Sheltonesque mystique that defines the work of Jeff Shelton.

(Following pages) The beamed ceilings and whitewashed walls of the interior spaces of El Andaluz express a modernism not apparent from the exterior elevations of the complex.

Malibu Classic

Architect: Erik Evens

Build: 2013

Location: Malibu, California

Architect Erik Evens is a classicist at heart, inspired from the outset through his studied inquiry of the architectural traditions of the United States, Europe, North Africa, and the Mediterranean. A native of Los Angeles, Evens completed his studies in architecture at Cal Poly San Luis Obispo, learning the great traditions of Europe and the Americas in the shadows of the early California Spanish mission of San Luis Obispo. However, despite working with a host of design firms, "It was his tenure in the Los Angeles office of Marc Appleton that sealed his passion for historical styles attuned to the classical principles of harmony, proportion, order, and, above all, beauty." There, he grew to embrace both traditional and classical design, and in 2013 branched off and established his own design firm. An independent design studio operating under the umbrella of the KAA Design Group based in Los Angeles, Evens Architects specializes in traditional and classically inspired homes and estates. With a flair for conjuring the eclecticism inherent in the traditions of the Mediterranean, Evens created this 2013 design and build in that Malibu is clearly the result of an inspired vision for capturing Andalusia and the Mediterranean in a premier Southern California venue.

(Right) Bricked groin vaults and an Andalusian hearth form the nucleus of this grand loggia in Malibu, California.

(*Above*) The loggia, landscaping, patios, and pool all function harmoniously to encourage engagement with the great outdoors.

(*Opposite, top*) Beamed ceilings, hardwood flooring, and a multitude of windows complement the spaciousness of this conjoined kitchen and dining area.

(*Opposite, bottom left*) The copper tub and adjoining balcony promise many an opportunity for moments of rest and relaxation.

(*Opposite, bottom right*) A wondrous chandelier and the panoramic view of the countryside are to be had in this first-floor getaway.

The extent to which Evens has achieved his vision for infusing Classicism into the contemporary homes of Southern California was validated of late in his having been awarded the 2019 LUXE Residential Excellence in Design Awards for this Malibu estate. The category, not unsurprisingly, "Regional Winner, Classic Architecture." The award specifically called out the fact that "Guests experience a sequence of outdoor rooms at this Malibu, California, family home, which engages the landscape in ways that encourage daily living outdoors."

Located at the epicenter of Point Dume in Malibu, the fenestration on all sides of this Mediterranean Revival home is dominated by a multitude of window types and sizes that afford spectacular views of the Pacific coast on three sides, and the Coast Ranges to the north. Whereas sunrise can be appreciated from the vantage point of the outdoor fireplace and vaulted masonry loggia overlooking the pool to the east, the light of the setting sun streams through the windows of the main facade into the rooms on the west. The spacious dimensions of the pointed, or lancet, window at the

east elevation clearly defines one of the most unique features of this home. With terracotta roof and floor tiles, vaulted arcades, beautifully handcrafted solid-wood doors, beamed cathedral ceilings, colorfully-tiled staircases, wrought-iron balconies and chandeliers, a luxuriously landscaped walled forecourt, and elaborately turned wrought-iron banisters and railings throughout. Through the towering iron gates that greet guests at the perimeter of the rock-wall enclosure that defines the forecourt, one is greeted by Persian rugs, wrought-iron wall sconces, period-appropriate furnishings, and the interplay of light and shadow that defines one's path through this magnificent home.

(Following pages) Sunset over Malibu and the Pacific Ocean.

Sloan Residence

Architect: Kevin A. Clark

Build: 2013

Location: Montecito, California

Majestic views of the Pacific define the ambience and character of this Spanish Colonial Revival home by renowned California architect Kevin A. Clark. Working with the site's greatest asset, "its off the hook views of the ocean" and Coast Ranges, Clark and his team were driven to transform this hill of enchantments into an impeccably designed single-family refuge. As with another Clark design and build, El Sueño in Santa Monica, similar priorities were at work in defining the eloquence of the Andalusian design scheme proposed. The atmospheric qualities of the home of Scott and Brittany Sloan are ultimately the product of a residential design that drew inspiration from the golden age of Spanish Colonial revivals, while at the same time developing features deemed from the outset as more practical to the needs of a modern-day family. The Sloans' considerable enthusiasm, diligence, and trust in the outcome permitted Clark to elaborate on those design priorities that effectively define the home's most enduring qualities. In the final analysis, these qualities were validated on the day the Sloans introduced their newborn into this warm and inviting, yet intimate and luxurious, newfound home setting.

(*Right*) The loggia affords majestic views of the Coast Ranges and their storied landscapes.

One of those features deemed most critical to the architect's design plan was that of the natural topography, including the escarpment at the rear of the residence that permitted the elaboration of Clark's hardscape design. For him, the topography of the lot was akin to a gift, in that it permitted the introduction of gardens and landscape features that clearly enhanced the qualities of the viewshed. To achieve their shared vision, Clark and the Sloans saw through the demolition of the preexisting residence, thereby opening the landscape to a new vision for this Spanish Colonial Revival. Drawing from the contours and available vistas, the home gradually took shape with a team that included interior designer Thomas C. Achille, and landscape architects Roland Crighton and Marc Diemer.

With the home's main facade oriented to the south and the winter sun, Clark and his team maximized the capture of both direct and ambient light and thereby the essential warmth, intimacy, and yet vibrant qualities of this new build. With authenticity as a main-stay of his designs, Clark integrated elements and features of the Andalusian and Spanish Colonial Revival styles that lend themselves to a redeeming sense of nostalgia for the glory days of early Hollywood and Southern California. According to Clark, one of his favorite, albeit most challenging, design features of the home was that of the incomparable semicircular corner balcony, replete with a classically inspired funnel or sconce-like form.

The asymmetrical floor plan, gleaming white stucco, terracotta-roof tiles, colonnades, wrought-iron balustrades, wooden balconies, coffered ceilings, and artistry of the hardscape design and drought-tolerant plantings all lend themselves to the beauty of the incomparable golden hues generated by the setting sun atop this enchanted hill overlooking the majesty of the Pacific coast of California.

(Opposite, top left) The colonnaded loggia constitutes a central feature of the Sloan residence.

(Opposite, bottom left) The circular exterior balcony is one of the architect's favorite features of this home.

(Left) Terracotta tiles, archways, whitewashed walls, and enclosed balconies are key to the Spanish Colonial Revival character of this residence.

(Above, left) Wrought-iron banisters, hardwood steps, whitewashed archways, and beamed ceilings all coalesce at this juncture.

(Above, right) Beamed ceilings, arches, and an Andalusian hearth enhance the identity of the living room.

(Following pages) Sunset over Montecito and the Santa Ynez Mountains.

Santa Barbara Walking Tour

Architect: Jeff Shelton

Build: (Various) 2002, 2008, 2014

Location: Santa Barbara, California

Drawing on the inspiration of Catalan architect Antoni Gaudí (1852–1926) and the beauty and sophistication, geometry and vibrant colors of Andalusian architecture, Santa Barbara's very own Jeff Shelton of Jeff Shelton Architect has advanced Gaudí's vision for Catalan modernism into Southern California. With organic forms, curvilinear wrought-iron and other fluid design elements, a proliferation of multicolored tiles and mosaics, and a surrealistic landscape of architectural elements, Jeff Shelton has created and/or redesigned a host of buildings in downtown Santa Barbara such that a "Sheltonesque" walking tour now defines the area. Area media have since christened Shelton's creations in terms of "stylishly whimsical designs" derived of liberal infusions of Gaudí, M. C. Escher, and Dr. Seuss, while clearly the subtext speaks to the traditions of *al-Andaluz*.

An appreciation for the colorfully whimsical and eccentric, albeit architecturally sophisticated, creations of Jeff Shelton is surely to be had by way of the walking tour of Santa Barbara buildings designed by Jeff Shelton. Shelton's own website features a colorfully rendered map of the tour. Jeff's mapping of the walking tour is bounded by Canon Perdido Street on the northwest, Chapala Street to the southwest, Highway 101 on the southeast, and Garden Street on the northeast. The recommended point of departure is that defined by the *Casa Blanca* off of State Street

(Top) Wrought-iron banisters and colorful azulejo tiles dominate this stairway.

(Bottom) Colorful azulejo glazed tiles are products of Jeff Shelton's design studios.

and Gutierrez Street. The Casa Blanca Restaurant on State Street is lavishly designed and furnished, and exudes a Sheltonesque exuberance à la Gaudí. Replete with colorfully tiled flooring, *zellij*-like wainscoting, Islamic archways, undulating arcades, Escher-like design elements, serpentine wood railings, flamboyant wrought-iron lamps and chandeliers, and engraved and finely cut sheet-metal panels, Shelton's inspiration is clearly evident.

Having begun the tour at Casa Blanca, the pilgrim is then directed to the Pistachio House near the corner of State and Gutierrez streets. Completed in the spring of 2002, this Shelton creation was awarded the George Washington Smith Award by the Architectural Board of Review and Historic Landmarks Commission in 2003. With its eclectic admixture of Andalusian, Moroccan, Gaudí, and Sheltonesque innovations, this private residence stands as unique, particularly in its use of both tile and metalwork. Moreover, its colorful canopied loggia, and the addition of four tiled-masonry "rugs" hung from the second-floor balcony add to the charm of this unique creation in the heart of Santa Barbara.

(Left) The whimsical character of Shelton's design schemes are enhanced by the judicious use of glazed tile, wrought-iron, and an exuberant color palette.

From the Pistachio House, the third Shelton build on the walking tour is that of Ablitt Tower on West Haley. Built in 2006, the tower is unique in virtually every way, and features stunning views of the mountains, riviera, and ocean. In effect, it is a work of art, although it was redesignated a hotel in 2017. Constructed from the ground up by Jeff Shelton and builder Dan Upton of Dan Upton, Construction, the seemingly improbable origins of a residential tower in downtown Santa Barbara took root on a 20-by-20-foot lot. After some four years of battling through a maze of town hall meetings and city building codes, Shelton and his team constructed a 53-foot tall tower consisting of 72 steps spanning four risers, and including 57 windows of every imaginable shape and size. Ultimately, the $1 million price tag produced 699 square feet of living space on a 19-by-19-foot footprint, excluding the rooftop patio. Each of those signature features noted in other Shelton designs along the tour are repeated here, although the wondrous sheet metal and wrought-iron craftsmanship of Jeff's brother David Shelton of David Shelton's Iron Shop, are prominently featured in this exuberant and unique building for the ages.

(Top) Shelton's design schemes have been characterized as Shelton-esque, or a hybrid melding of Gaudí, Escher, and Seuss.

(Bottom) Shelton's creations encompass a range of products, including custom time and metal designs.

El Andaluz constitutes the fourth stop along the walking tour, and is among the most exuberant and innovative of those designs along the pathway featuring Shelton's creations. Fronting Chapala Street, this sizable condominium complex embodies many of those Andalusian elements identified in other Sheltonesque works. El Andaluz is notable for the

extent to which elements identified with the *Mezquita,* or Mosque-Cathedral of Córdoba, were integrated. In addition to the iconic horseshoe-shaped arches that grace the main facade and exault the exoticism of the arcade, the two buildings are joined by a bridgeway, or second-floor wood-framed room-block that emulates the *meshrebeeyeh* or enclosed balconies of many a Muslim town. The coffered ceiling formed beneath the bridge way in turn features an elaborate *artesonado* or adorned ceiling comprised of several woods. The interior courtyard is rich with elaborately tiled fountains, flooring, stairways, corridors, archways, and artfully designed sheet or plate-metal balconies, arcades, and balustrades. Virtually all of the brightly pigmented tilework is the product of Shelton's team of roving artisans and craftsmen and -women, and the Jeff Shelton Tile Collection at Villa Lagoon Tile.

From the flamboyance of El Andaluz, the walking tour crosses Chapala Street and winds it way past *David Shelton Design,* formerly *Shelton's Iron Shop,* on Fig Avenue at the corner of Cota Street. Adjacent to the iron shop on Fig Avenue are the offices of *Jeff Shelton Architect,* and just beyond follows the elaborately festooned *Vera Cruz,* a private live-work

(Left) Miraculously, Shelton designed and constructed the Ablitt residential tower on a 20-foot-by-20-foot floor plan in 2007.

residential venue. The colorful facade of this home consists of a floor to gable mosaic of paintings created, assembled, and installed by Shelton and artist Richard Wilke, with the assistance of other local artists invited by Shelton to contribute to this constellation of painted panels forming the facade. Shelton's design in this instance was inspired by the since-demolished House of a Thousand Paintings. From Vera Cruz, the eighth stop on the walking tour is that of *El Zapato* on Garden Street near the corner of Haley Street.

Built in 2014, El Zapato features some of the most colorful and flamboyant purple sheet-metal forms and brightly colored yellow-and-red-ochre-tile archways identified with the main elevation of this particularly ornate building. Shaped like a boot, the three-story tower at the northwest end of the elevation is conjoined to a single-story elevation with a horseshoe-shaped archway leading into the courtyard. In this instance, virtually every window piercing is adorned with full or partial custom-tile surrounds, and features a prominent curvilinear wrought-iron balcony and bright orange, yellow, and black canopies with wrought-iron rods. The exteriors exude the flair of Andalusian elements found in southern Spain, while the interiors are beautifully appointed and styled so as to accent the interplay of light and shadow throughout.

Like each of the aforementioned walking tour locations, the Gaudí-esque character and Andalusian ambience of Shelton's designs is particularly acute in the ninth and tenth stops along the tour. Whereas the Cota Street Studios on Cota and Garden streets incorporate a panoply of otherworldly sheet-metal doors and other ironworks by David Shelton Design, El Jardin on Garden Street completes the circuit with a majestic four-story Andalusian complex replete with twisted-iron railings, balconies, Escher-like stairways, richly tiled facades, and a host of arabesque elements germane to the works of this master craftsman.

(Right) The telltale signs of David Shelton's plate-metal craftsmanship are featured in virtually every possible configuration imaginable.

GLOSSARY

COMPILED BY LESLIE MOSQUEDA
AFTER HINTZEN-BOHLEN (2013), JEFFERY (2003) AND SCHUETZ-MILLER, (1994).

Ajarcas (Arabic *as-saraka*, "an interlacing bow"), a pattern of low relief resembling a trellis.

Ajimez (mullioned window), biforium windows of Gothic origins.

Alarife (Arabic, Sp. maestro de obras), master builder.

Alcázar (Arabic *a/-kasr*, "castle"): barricaded or walled Moorish palace.

Alfarje (Arabic *al farkh*, "a space between two things"), horizontal wooden beams, often decorated with patterns.

Alfiz (Andalusian Arabic *alhíz*, from *alháyyiz*, "a container"), rectangular architectural molding enclosing outward portion of an arch.

Aplantillado, mosaiclike or patterned brickwork.

Arabesque (Fr. arabesque, "Arabic ornamentation"; *arabesco*, "Arabic"), decorative intertwined leaves and vines.

Arcade (Fr. arcade, "strainer arch"; Lat. *arcus*, "arch, bow"), enclosed walkway with rows of arches placed on piers or columns.

Armadura (Sp. armazón, sostén, framework), timber framework or roofing armature.

Artesonado (Sp. "paneling," Spanish *arteson*), inverted shape of exposed wooden roof, or adorned ceiling comprised of several woods, positioned to create geometric patterns.

Ataurique, repetitive decorative motif comprised of vegetal or floral patterns inherent to Islamic Spain and North African design.

Azulejería (from the Arabic *az-zulai*, "ornamental tile"), art of varnished tilework.

Azulejos (Sp.; from azul, "blue"; Arab. *az-zuleycha*, "glazed, colored stoneware"), colorful, glazed tiles made from fired clay.

Baroque (from Port. *barocco*, "little stone, irregularly round"), European architecture of the seventeenth and eighteenth centuries characterized by ornate detail.

Barrel vault, ceiling cross-section is usually an arc; rarely composed of a pointed or parabolic cross section.

Bóveda (Sp. techo curvo, cúpula), masonry vault, dome, cupola.

Bóveda esquifada, octagonal or eight-sided diagonal dome.

Charbagh (*Chahar Bagh*), a quadrilateral garden layout identified with the four gardens and water features of the Islamic paradise described in the Quran.

Coffering, inner area of an arch or ceiling with a rectangular, box shaped recessed panels.

Compound pier, a group of small and large columns arranged around a core pillar.

Corinthian column, similar to Ionic columns with richly shaped base and a slim shaft fluted with fillets; its capital and abacus, however, are decorated with acanthus leaves (large prickly thistle-type leaves curled up at the tips).

Crenellation, a rectangular barrier on top of a wall, often placed in a row.

Cuenca (Sp.), *azulejo* (colorful, glazed tile) with (clay) fillets to border the individual ornamental fields.

Dome, a ceiling or roof arched above a round, rectangular or polygonal base.

Drum, circular architectural area between the building and the dome, often used to raise the height of the building.

Empedrado (nm, Sp., suelo revestido de piedras), Andalusian pebble paving or stone pavement.

Entablature, uppermost part of one of the orders of architecture.

Espadaña, extension of a wall, pierced with arches to hang bells.

Frieze (Med. Lat. *frisium*, "Phrygian work" or "fringe"), sculptural continuous wall adornment in a straight format.

Frontispiece (Fr. *frontispice*, "front side [of a building]"), three-sided pediment above the front of a building's doors and windows.

Garth, an open quadrangle, also called a *patio*.

Hammam (hamam, hamán, nm; baño arabe), bathhouse, Turkish baths.

Horseshoe arch, arc-shaped semicircle that narrows at the base.

Intrados, interior surface of an arch.

Isabelline style (Sp. *estilo lsaben*), stylistic term named after Isabella I (1451–1504), often identified through exhibiting rampant flamboyant (flame ornament) forms with some *Mudéjar* elements.

Laceria, interweaving of bands in geometric pattern composing polygons.

Latillas, wooden ceiling consisting of intertwined of small poles spanning beams or *varas*.

Mashrabiya (Arabic root *sharab*, "to drink," also *Meshrebeeyeh*), a projecting oriel window or window screen consisting of lattice or wood panels carved to express a geometric pattern.

Mudéjar (adj., ES relativo a musulmanes), a subject Muslim during the Christian reconquest of the Iberian peninsula; Iberian Gothic and Islamic architectural style of the twelfth to fifteenth centuries.

Muqarnas or Mocárabe (Arabic "joining together"), archetypal or vernacular form of ornamented vaulting consisting of triangular projections or connecting tiers or segments in Islamic architecture.

Neoclassicism (from Fr. *classique* and Lat. *classicus*, "exemplary"), architectural style derived from the works of classical antiquity, and in vogue in France and Italy in the mid-eighteenth century.

Niche, a hollowed area of a wall or *retablo* in which to present a religious image.

Pendentive (Fr. "suspended arch"), a curved three-sided area utilized to connect a square ground plan with the round dome atop.

Plateresque style (Sp. *platero*, "silversmith"), stylistic term used for Spanish architectural and decorative art.

Portico (Lat. *porticus*, "arcade, hall"), often-open structure supported by columns or pillars, placed in front of the main entrance to a building.

Reticulated vault, a term used to describe the ribs to form a network to camouflage the division of the structure.

Rib vault, the crossing of two barrel vaults of equal size; such crossings are called ribs.

Rill (Sp. *riachuelo* nm, *arroyuelo*, *arroyito* nm, En. small stream), Islamic Spain or North African linear water feature.

Sebka, diamond-shaped, crisscross ornamentation introduced by the Almohads.

Star vault, vault in which the ribs form a star pattern.

Vigas, wooden beams, at times carved and painted.

Yeseria (Sp. "plaster"), carved plaster or stucco featuring geometric or floral motifs.

Zaguán (Arabic *ustawaan*, "porch, breezeway"), open space hidden from the public eye.

Zapatas, carved and corbelled wooden brackets.

Zellij or zellige (Arabic): Moroccan and Al-Andaluz mosaic tilework designed from individually chiseled geometric tiles set into a plaster base.

REFERENCES

Barrucand, Marianne, and Achim Bednorz. *Moorish Architecture in Andalusia*. Köln: Taschen, 2002.

Beebe, Rose Marie, and Robert M. Senkewicz. *Junípero Serra: California, Indians, and the Transformation of a Missionary*. Norman: University of Oklahoma Press, 2015.

Danby, Miles. *Moorish Style*. London: Phaidon, 1995.

Dodds, J. *Architecture and Ideology in Early Medieval Spain*. Philadelphia: Pennsylvania State University Press, 1994.

Grist, Julie. "Ruskin Art Club Reborn as Historic Home in Windsor Village." http://www.larchmontbuzz.com/larchmont-village-life/ruskin-art-club-reborn-home-windsor-village. January 13, 2015.

Haldeman, Peter. Grounded in Tradition: In Beverly Hills, A New House Evokes The Spanish Colonial Revival With a Feel For Today. Photography by Mary E. Nichols. *Architectural Digest*, pp. 280–287, October 2006.

Haldeman, Peter. "Look Inside a Mediterranean-Style Residence in Los Angeles." Photography by Simon Upton. *Architectural Digest*, April 2011.

Hintzen-Bohlen, Brigitte. *Andalusia: Art & Architecture*. Potsdam: H.F. Ullmann, 2013.

Jeffery, R. "From Azulejos to Zaguanes: The Islamic Legacy in the Built Environment of Hispano-America." *Journal of the Southwest, 45*(2003), 289–327.

Mann, Vivian B., Thomas F. Glick, and Jerrilynn Denise Dodds (eds.). Convivencia: *Jews, Muslims, and Christians in Medieval Spain*. New York: George Braziller, 1992.

Mendoza, Rubén G., and Jennifer A. Lucido. Of Earth, Fire, and Faith: Architectural Practice in the Fernandino Missions of Alta California, 1769-1821. In *Colonial Latin American Historical Review*. Spring, 2014, pp. 1-47. Albuquerque: University of New Mexico

Mendoza, Rubén G., and Melba Levick. *The California Missions*. Text by Rubén G. Mendoza, and photography by Melba Levick. New York: Rizzoli, 2018.

Newcomb, Rexford, *Mediterranean Domestic Architecture in the United States*, Cleveland: J. H. Jansen, 1928, p. 4.

Schuetz-Miller, M. *Building and Builders in Hispanic California, 1769–1850*. Tucson, Arizona: Santa Barbara, California: Southwestern Mission Research Center; Santa Barbara Trust for Historic Preservation, 1994.

ACKNOWLEDGMENTS

We gratefully acknowledge the many institutions, architects, designers, homeowners, representatives, and staff who gave of their time and attention to our many editorial requests and site visits. Each of them is heir to the grand architectural traditions of Andalusia, North Africa, and the Spanish style in the Americas. This book would not have come to fruition without the vision and commitment of our publisher, Charles Miers, our editor, Douglas Curran, and the book's designer, Scott Gross. We are forever grateful to the Rizzoli team, and in particular to Douglas for his keen aesthetic eye, design contributions, unflagging leadership, and promotion of this labor of love.

Melba Levick extends a special thanks to Matt Walla for his invaluable and expert technical assistance. Mendoza is particularly indebted to CSU Monterey Bay Adjunct Professor Jennifer A. Lucido for her thoroughgoing critique, supplementary research, and editorial feedback for all content generated from the outset, and to Sr. Pablo Ybarra of the Asociación Blas de Lezo, Memoria de la Hispanidad, who facilitated access to the grand estates of Andalusia, Spain. Estate owners Enrique Moreno de la Cova and Cristina Ybarra proved exceptionally generous in provisioning contacts in Andalusia, while permitting access to and photography of the Palacio de Portocarrero in Palma del Río, Spain. Mendoza is particularly indebted to CSU Monterey Bay Archaeology Program student Leslie Mosqueda for her diligent scholarship and contributions to the development of the glossary.

Melba Levick and Rubén Mendoza gratefully acknowledge the following people, who in one way or another helped make this book possible: Diane Wilk and Michael Burch, Stuart Denenberg, Crosby Doe, Gabriel Meyer, April Palmer, Josie and Doug Smith, and Mary Sweeney. We are particularly indebted to California architects Marc Appleton, Tom Callaway, Kevin Clark, Erik Evens, Henry Lenny, Jeff Shelton, Robert Sinclair, and Raun and Brian Tichenor, who have been exceptionally generous with their time, and have provided many fruitful leads and suggestions. These same architects afforded us access to their own wonderfully inspired homes, several of which grace these pages. We are particularly grateful to all those who graciously opened their homes to us for this book. In Andalusia, photographer Wayne Chasan proved particularly generous with his contacts, and assisted Melba with mapping her trip through Andalusia. Manuel Domecq provisioned access to the Domecq Palace. Carmen Jiménez-Alfaro, Condesa de Prado Castellano, facilitated a wonderful day of photography at her beautiful estate, the Casa Palacio de Cardenas in Écija. In addition, the Condesa facilitated introductions to the owners of other exceptional venues and *palacios* in Andalusia. Melba also wishes to thank Susana Marin, and Anthony and Patrick Reid of the Hacienda de San Rafael and Corral del Rey, and the Hotel Monasterio de San Francisco in Palma Del Rio. Jose Manuel Arnal Perez of the Hotel San Gabriel, Ronda, Abi Quesada of the Hotel Carmen de los Chapiteles, and Eduardo Shelly of the Casa Shelly in Vejer de la Frontera, who afforded Melba wonderful stays in their respective hotels, while at the same time facilitating area photo shoots. Archaeologist Pilar Delgado Blasco conducted a particularly rich and informative tour of the *Baños arabes*, and entry to the Mondragon Archaeology Museum in Ronda. Alphonso Prado, Director of RealMaester Ronda, kindly arranged site visits to the *palacios* and the *Plaza de Toros de Ronda*, and Rafa Porras facilitated guidance and access to the most beautiful patios of Córdoba.

Finally, the coauthors acknowledge their respective families. To that end, Rubén Mendoza expresses his gratitude for the loving support of his wife, Linda Marie, and the infinite patience and understanding of his talented daughters, Natalie Marie and Maya Nicole Mendoza. Melba Levick in turn wishes to acknowledge and thank her devoted husband, Hugh Levick, without whose patience, assistance and support this book would not have been possible.